P9-DOE-836

NO FEAR SHAKESPEARE

HENRY V

SPARK NOTES

Copyright © 2004 by Spark Publishing

All rights reserved. No part of this book may be used or reproduced in any manner whatsoever without the written permission of the Publisher.

SPARKNOTES is a registered trademark of SparkNotes LLC

The original text and translation for this edition were prepared by John Crowther.

Spark Publishing
120 Fifth Avenue
New York, NY 10011
www.sparknotes.com

Please submit all comments and questions or report errors to *www.sparknotes.com/errors*

07 08 09 **SN** 10 9

Printed and bound in the United States

ISBN-13: 978-1-4114-0103-7
ISBN-10: 1-4114-0103-4

Library of Congress Cataloging-in-Publication Data

Shakespeare, William, 1564–1616.
Henry V / edited by John Crowther.
p. cm. — (No fear Shakespeare)
ISBN 1-4114-0103-4
1. Henry V, King of England, 1387–1422—Drama. 2. Great Britain—History—Henry V, 1413–1422—Drama. I. Crowther, John (John C.) II. Title.
PR2812.A2C76 2004
822.3'3—dc22

2004009851

There's matter in these sighs, these profound heaves.
You must translate: 'tis fit we understand them.

(*Hamlet*, 4.1.1–2)

FEAR NOT.

Have you ever found yourself looking at a Shakespeare play, then down at the footnotes, then back at the play, and still not understanding? You know what the individual words mean, but they don't add up. SparkNotes' *No Fear Shakespeare* will help you break through all that. Put the pieces together with our easy-to-read translations. Soon you'll be reading Shakespeare's own words fearlessly—and actually enjoying it.

No Fear Shakespeare puts Shakespeare's language side-by-side with a facing-page translation into modern English—the kind of English people actually speak today. When Shakespeare's words make your head spin, our translation will help you sort out what's happening, who's saying what, and why.

NO FEAR SHAKESPEARE

As You Like It

The Comedy of Errors

Hamlet

Henry IV, Parts One and Two

Henry V

Julius Caesar

King Lear

Macbeth

The Merchant of Venice

A Midsummer Night's Dream

Much Ado About Nothing

Othello

Richard III

Romeo and Juliet

Sonnets

The Taming of the Shrew

The Tempest

Twelfth Night

HENRY V

CHARACTERS

Chorus—A single character who introduces each of the play's five acts. Like the group of singers who constituted the chorus in Greek drama, the Chorus in *Henry V* offers commentary on the play's plot and themes.

King Henry V—The young, recently crowned king of England. Henry is brilliant, focused, fearless, and committed to the responsibilities of kingship. These responsibilities often force him to place his personal feelings second to the needs of the crown. Henry is a brilliant orator who uses his skill to justify his claims and to motivate his troops. Once Henry has resolved to conquer France, he pursues his goal relentlessly to the end.

The Dukes of Exeter, Westmorland, Salisbury, and **Warwick**—Trusted advisors to King Henry and the leaders of his military. The Duke of Exeter, who is also Henry's uncle, is entrusted with carrying important messages to the French king.

The Dukes of Clarence, Bedford, and **Gloucester**—Henry's three younger brothers. Clarence, Bedford, and Gloucester are noblemen and fighters.

The Archbishop of Canterbury and **the Bishop of Ely**—Wealthy and powerful English clergymen. The Archbishop of Canterbury and the Bishop of Ely do not go to fight in the war, but their urging and fund-raising are important factors in Henry's initial decision to invade France.

Cambridge, Scrope, and **Grey**—Three conspirators against King Henry. Cambridge, Scrope, and Grey are bribed by French agents to kill Henry before he sets sail for France. Scrope's betrayal of his king is particularly surprising, as Scrope and Henry are good friends.

York and **Suffolk**—Two noble cousins who die together at the Battle of Agincourt.

The King of France—Charles VI. A capable leader, Charles does not underestimate King Henry, as his son, the Dauphin, does.

Isabel—The queen of France, married to Charles VI. Isabel does not appear until the final scene, in which her daughter, Catherine, is betrothed to King Henry.

The Dauphin—The son of the king of France and heir to the French throne. The Dauphin is a headstrong and overconfident young man, more inclined to mock the English than to make preparations to fight them. He also mocks Henry, making frequent mention of the king's irresponsible youth.

Catherine—The daughter of the king of France. Catherine is eventually married off to King Henry in order to cement the peace between England and France. She speaks little English.

French noblemen and military leaders—The Constable of France, the Duke of Orléans, the Duke of Britain, the Duke of Bourbon, the Earl of Grandpré, Lord Rambures, the Duke of Burgundy, and the Governor of Harfleur are French noblemen and military leaders. Like the Dauphin, most of these leaders are more interested in making jokes about the English than in taking them seriously as a fighting force.

Sir Thomas Erpingham—A wise, aged veteran of many wars who serves with Henry's campaign.

Captain Gower—An army captain and a capable fighter who serves with Henry's campaign.

Captain Fluellen, Captain MacMorris, and **Captain Jamy**—The captains of King Henry's troops from Wales, Ireland, and Scotland, respectively, all of whom have heavy accents reflecting their countries of origin. Fluellen, a close friend of Captain Gower, is the most prominent of the three. His wordiness provides comic relief, but he is an intelligent leader and strategist.

Ancient Pistol—A commoner from London who serves in the war with Henry, and a friend of Nim and Bardolph. Pistol speaks with a blustery and melodramatic poetic diction; he is married to the hostess of the Boar's Head Tavern in London.

Bardolph—A commoner from London who serves in the war with Henry, and a friend of Pistol and Nim. Bardolph is a former friend of King Henry from his wild youth. A thief and a coward, Bardolph gets into trouble for looting from the conquered towns in violation of the king's order.

Nim—A commoner from London who serves in the war with Henry, and a friend of Pistol and Bardolph.

Boy—Formerly in the service of Falstaff, the nameless boy leaves London after his master's death and goes with Pistol, Nim, and Bardolph to the war in France. The boy is touchy and embarrassed that his companions are cowardly thieves.

Michael Williams, John Bates, and **Alexander Court**—Common soldiers with whom King Henry, disguised, argues the night before the Battle of Agincourt. Though he argues at length with Williams, King Henry is generally impressed with these men's intelligence and courage.

Hostess—The keeper of the Boar's Head Tavern in London. Mistress Quickly, as she is also known, is married to Pistol.

Alice—The maid of the French princess Catherine. Alice has spent time in England and teaches Catherine some English, though not very well.

Montjoy—The French herald, or messenger.

Monsieur le Fer—A French soldier and gentleman who is captured by Pistol at the Battle of Agincourt.

NO FEAR SHAKESPEARE

HENRY V

ACT ONE

PROLOGUE

Enter CHORUS

CHORUS

Oh, for a muse of fire that would ascend
The brightest heaven of invention!
A kingdom for a stage, princes to act,
And monarchs to behold the swelling scene!
Then should the warlike Harry, like himself,
Assume the port of Mars, and at his heels,
Leashed in like hounds, should famine, sword, and fire
Crouch for employment. But pardon, gentles all,
The flat unraisèd spirits that hath dared
On this unworthy scaffold to bring forth
So great an object. Can this cockpit hold
The vasty fields of France? Or may we cram
Within this wooden *O* the very casques
That did affright the air at Agincourt?
O pardon, since a crookèd figure may
Attest in little place a million,
And let us, ciphers to this great account,
On your imaginary forces work.
Suppose within the girdle of these walls
Are now confined two mighty monarchies
Whose high uprearèd and abutting fronts
The perilous narrow ocean parts asunder.
Piece out our imperfections with your thoughts.
Into a thousand parts divide one man,
And make imaginary puissance.
Think, when we talk of horses, that you see them
Printing their proud hoofs i' th' receiving earth,
For 'tis your thoughts that now must deck our kings,
Carry them here and there, jumping o'er times,

ACT ONE

PROLOGUE

The CHORUS *enters.*

CHORUS

If only we had divine inspiration, our play might rise to the highest level of imagination. If we had a stage as big as a kingdom, real kings and queens to act the part of kings and queens, and royalty to also witness the glorious spectacle, then it would be as it really was. Then valiant King Harry would resemble the god of war, as he did in life, and famine, sword, and fire would sit like dogs at his feet, waiting to be unleashed. But, ladies and gentlemen, since that's not the case, you must forgive us plain, ordinary men who dare to act out so great a story on this humble stage. Can this theater seem to contain the sweeping fields of France? Could we even squeeze into this little theater the helmets that looked so frightening at Agincourt? Hardly! But, pardon us, because just as a few strokes of a pen, a few zeros, can signify a huge number, we, who are zeros in this great story, can work on your imagination. Pretend that within the confines of this theater sit two great kingdoms divided by a narrow but perilous ocean. Let your thoughts make up for our imperfections. Divide each man into a thousand, and there you will have an imaginary army. Imagine, when we talk of horses, that you see them planting their proud hooves in the soft earth. Because now it is your thoughts that must dress up our kings and transport them from place to place. Your thoughts must leap over huge spans of time, turning the events of many

Turning th' accomplishment of many years
Into an hour-glass; for the which supply,
Admit me chorus to this history;
Who, prologue-like, your humble patience pray
Gently to hear, kindly to judge our play.

Exit

years into the space of a few hours. To that end, consider me a sort of chorus, here to help tell the story. And, as the speaker of any prologue should, I ask you to hear our play courteously and to judge it kindly.

The CHORUS *exits.*

ACT 1, SCENE 1

Enter the Archbishop of CANTERBURY *and the Bishop of* ELY

CANTERBURY

My lord, I'll tell you that self bill is urged
Which in th' eleventh year of the last king's reign
Was like, and had indeed against us passed
But that the scambling and unquiet time
Did push it out of farther question.

ELY

But how, my lord, shall we resist it now?

CANTERBURY

It must be thought on. If it pass against us,
We lose the better half of our possession,
For all the temporal lands which men devout
By testament have given to the Church
Would they strip from us, being valued thus:
"As much as would maintain, to the King's honor,
Full fifteen earls and fifteen hundred knights,
Six thousand and two hundred good esquires;
And, to relief of lazars and weak age
Of indigent faint souls past corporal toil,
A hundred almshouses right well supplied;
And to the coffers of the King besides,
A thousand pounds by th' year." Thus runs the bill.

ELY

This would drink deep.

CANTERBURY

'Twould drink the cup and all.

ELY

But what prevention?

CANTERBURY

The king is full of grace and fair regard.

ELY

And a true lover of the holy Church.

ACT 1, SCENE 1

The Archbishop of CANTERBURY *and the Bishop of* ELY *enter.*

CANTERBURY

My lord, this bill that's being proposed is the same one that was proposed in the eleventh year of old King Henry's reign. Everyone thought it would pass then, and it probably would have had it not been for the great civil unrest and uncertainty of the time, which required the matter to be put off.

ELY

But how will we keep it from being passed now, my lord?

CANTERBURY

We have to think about that. If it does pass, the Church will lose more than half of what it possesses, because the bill would strip us of enough real estate left to the church by wealthy, pious men in their wills to support fifteen earls and fifteen hundred knights, six thousand two hundred squires, and a hundred well-supplied almshouses for the relief of lepers, old-age pensioners, the poor, and those too weak or sick to work. Add to that a yearly sum of a thousand pounds to go directly into the king's coffers. That's what the bill says.

ELY

That would be quite a drain.

CANTERBURY

It would drain us dry.

ELY

But what can be done to prevent it?

CANTERBURY

The king is virtuous and kind.

CANTERBURY

The courses of his youth promised it not.
The breath no sooner left his father's body
But that his wildness, mortified in him,
Seemed to die too. Yea, at that very moment
Consideration like an angel came
And whipped th' offending Adam out of him,
Leaving his body as a paradise
T' envelop and contain celestial spirits.
Never was such a sudden scholar made,
Never came reformation in a flood
With such a heady currance scouring faults,
Nor never Hydra-headed willfulness
So soon did lose his seat, and all at once,
As in this king.

ELY

We are blessèd in the change.

CANTERBURY

Hear him but reason in divinity
And, all-admiring, with an inward wish,
You would desire the King were made a prelate.
Hear him debate of commonwealth affairs,
You would say it hath been all in all his study.
List his discourse of war, and you shall hear
A fearful battle rendered you in music.
Turn him to any cause of policy,
The Gordian knot of it he will unloose
Familiar as his garter; that, when he speaks,
The air, a chartered libertine, is still,
And the mute wonder lurketh in men's ears
To steal his sweet and honeyed sentences;
So that the art and practic part of life
Must be the mistress to this theoric;
Which is a wonder how his Grace should glean it,
Since his addiction was to courses vain,
His companies unlettered, rude, and shallow,

ELY

And a true lover of the holy Church.

CANTERBURY

You wouldn't have expected it based on how he acted as a youth. But no sooner had his father stopped breathing than the prince's wildness died too. Really, at that precise moment he gained a capacity for reflection, which appeared like an angel to chase away the sinful part of him, leaving his body like a paradise, fit to house only lofty thoughts and feelings. You never saw anyone become serious and studious so quickly. You never saw such a total transformation, as though a wild river, rushing through, had swept away his faults. Such a collection of stubborn character flaws was never banished from one place so suddenly as in the case of this king.

ELY

We are fortunate in the change.

CANTERBURY

If you just listen to him discuss theological matters, you'll find yourself thinking privately what an excellent bishop he would make. Hear him debate matters of domestic policy, and you'd swear he had made them his constant study. Listen to him talk about war, and you'll hear elegant and thrilling accounts of the battles. Bring up any political topic, and he'll untangle it as easily as if it were his own garter. And the result is that when he speaks, the very air—which is free to go where it likes—stops dead, and men stand in silent wonder, hoping to catch the benefit of his gorgeous utterances. There must be skill and experience behind all this abstract thought, but it's anyone's guess how he obtained it, since in his youth he preferred shallow pursuits, with uneducated, crude and superficial companions. He spent his time drunken, overfed, and

A garter was a band used to hold up stockings or shirt sleeves.

His hours filled up with riots, banquets, sports,
And never noted in him any study,
Any retirement, any sequestration
From open haunts and popularity.

ELY

The strawberry grows underneath the nettle,
And wholesome berries thrive and ripen best
Neighbored by fruit of baser quality;
And so the Prince obscured his contemplation
Under the veil of wildness, which, no doubt,
Grew like the summer grass, fastest by night,
Unseen yet crescive in his faculty.

CANTERBURY

It must be so, for miracles are ceased,
And therefore we must needs admit the means
How things are perfected.

ELY

But, my good lord,
How now for mitigation of this bill
Urged by the Commons? Doth his Majesty
Incline to it or no?

CANTERBURY

He seems indifferent,
Or rather swaying more upon our part
Than cherishing th' exhibitors against us;
For I have made an offer to his Majesty—
Upon our spiritual convocation
And in regard of causes now in hand,
Which I have opened to his Grace at large,
As touching France—to give a greater sum
Than ever at one time the clergy yet
Did to his predecessors part withal.

ELY

How did this offer seem received, my lord?

constantly seeking out entertainment, with no inclination for learning or quiet contemplation, nor any limit to his tolerance for public haunts and crowds.

ELY

Strawberries grow underneath nettle plants, and berries grow best when they're planted next to inferior fruit. In the same way, the prince hid his serious side under the guise of wild behavior. Just like summer grass, which grows fastest during the night, this sober quality was able to grow and thrive all the better for being undetected.

CANTERBURY

That must be it, because the age of miracles is passed, and we have to find reasonable explanations for why these things happen.

ELY

But tell me, my lord: as to the softening of this bill proposed by the House of Commons, does his Majesty favor it or not?

CANTERBURY

He seems neutral, perhaps leaning a little more toward our side than that of our opponents—since I've made his Majesty an offer, following a meeting with our fellow bishops. The offer regards certain matters having to do with France that his Grace and I have been discussing. My offer would involve us giving him a greater sum than the clergy ever gave at one time to any of his predecessors.

ELY

How did he take the offer, my lord?

CANTERBURY

Favorably, except that there wasn't enough time for his Grace to hear, as I sensed he would have liked to,

CANTERBURY

With good acceptance of his Majesty—
Save that there was not time enough to hear,
As I perceived his Grace would fain have done,
The severals and unhidden passages
Of his true titles to some certain dukedoms,
And generally to the crown and seat of France,
Derived from Edward, his great-grandfather.

ELY

What was th' impediment that broke this off?

CANTERBURY

The French ambassador upon that instant
Craved audience. And the hour, I think, is come
To give him hearing. Is it four o'clock?

ELY

It is.

CANTERBURY

Then go we in to know his embassy,
Which I could with a ready guess declare
Before the Frenchman speak a word of it.

ELY

I'll wait upon you, and I long to hear it.

Exeunt

the details about how he is rightfully entitled to certain dukedoms in France, and to the throne of France in general, through clear lines of descent originating with his great-grandfather, Edward III.

ELY

What kept you from telling him this?

CANTERBURY

The French ambassador arrived at that moment and asked to see the king. And, in fact, I think they're meeting together right now. Is it four o'clock?

ELY

It is.

CANTERBURY

Then let's go in and hear what he has to say—though I think I can guess before the Frenchman has uttered a word.

ELY

I'll accompany you. I'm also eager to hear it.

They exit.

ACT 1, SCENE 2

Enter KING HENRY, GLOUCESTER, BEDFORD, EXETER, WARWICK, WESTMORELAND, *and attendants*

KING HENRY
Where is my gracious lord of Canterbury?

EXETER
Not here in presence.

KING HENRY
Send for him, good uncle.

WESTMORELAND
Shall we call in th' ambassador, my liege?

KING HENRY
Not yet, my cousin. We would be resolved,
Before we hear him, of some things of weight
That task our thoughts concerning us and France.

Enter the Archbishop of CANTERBURY *and the Bishop of* ELY

CANTERBURY
God and his angels guard your sacred throne
And make you long become it.

KING HENRY
Sure we thank you.
My learnèd lord, we pray you to proceed
And justly and religiously unfold
Why the law Salic that they have in France
Or should or should not bar us in our claim.
And God forbid, my dear and faithful lord,
That you should fashion, wrest, or bow your reading,
Or nicely charge your understanding soul
With opening titles miscreate, whose right
Suits not in native colors with the truth;
For God doth know how many now in health
Shall drop their blood in approbation

ACT 1, SCENE 2

KING HENRY, GLOUCESTER, BEDFORD, EXETER, WARWICK, *and* WESTMORELAND *enter, with attendants.*

KING HENRY
Where is my gracious lord of Canterbury?

EXETER
He's not here.

KING HENRY
Send for him, dear uncle.

WESTMORELAND
Shall we call in the ambassador, my liege?

KING HENRY
Not yet, cousin. Before I hear him, I want to decide some important issues that are on my mind concerning my throne and France.

The archbishop of CANTERBURY *and the bishop of* ELY *enter.*

CANTERBURY
May God and his angels guard your sacred throne and grant that you dignify it for a long time.

KING HENRY
Thank you, I'm sure. My learned lord, kindly explain to us the legal and religious grounds for why this French Salic law either should or shouldn't bar me in my claim. And God forbid, my dear and faithful lord, that you should invent, twist, or distort your interpretation, or burden your conscience by subtly arguing for false claims. For God knows how many healthy men will shed their blood in support of whatever you persuade me to do. So think carefully before you incite

Of what your reverence shall incite us to.
Therefore take heed how you impawn our person,
How you awake our sleeping sword of war.
We charge you in the name of God, take heed,
For never two such kingdoms did contend
Without much fall of blood, whose guiltless drops
Are every one a woe, a sore complaint
'Gainst him whose wrong gives edge unto the swords
That make such waste in brief mortality.
Under this conjuration, speak, my lord,
For we will hear, note, and believe in heart
That what you speak is in your conscience washed
As pure as sin with baptism.

CANTERBURY
Then hear me, gracious sovereign, and you peers
That owe yourselves, your lives, and services
To this imperial throne. There is no bar
To make against your Highness' claim to France
But this, which they produce from Pharamond:
"*In terram Salicam mulieres ne succedant*"
(No woman shall succeed in Salic land),
Which Salic land the French unjustly gloze
To be the realm of France, and Pharamond
The founder of this law and female bar.
Yet their own authors faithfully affirm
That the land Salic is in Germany,
Between the floods of Sala and of Elbe,
Where Charles the Great, having subdued the Saxons,
There left behind and settled certain French,
Who, holding in disdain the German women
For some dishonest manners of their life,
Established then this law: to wit, no female
Should be inheritrix in Salic land,
Which "Salic," as I said, 'twixt Elbe and Sala
Is at this day in Germany called Meissen.

me to wage war. I charge you, in the name of God, be careful what you say. For mighty kingdoms such as England and France have never gone to war with one another without much bloodshed, every innocent drop of which cries out against the wrongdoer who caused such loss of life without good reason. With this in mind, speak, my lord. And I will listen, consider, and earnestly believe that what you say is spoken with a conscience as pure as a newly baptized soul.

CANTERBURY

Then hear me, gracious sovereign, and all you peers who owe your lives and duty to this imperial throne. There is no legal obstacle to your Highness's claim to France except the following rule, which the French cite from King Pharamond: *In terram Salicam mulieres ne succedant* (No woman shall inherit property in the Salic land). The French wrongly interpret "the Salic land" to mean France, and they cite Pharamond as the founder of this law that bars female succession to the throne. But their own authors assert that the Salic land is in Germany, between the Sala and the Elbe rivers, where Charles the Great left behind certain French settlements after conquering the Saxons. The French settlers despised the German women because they were unfaithful to their husbands, so the settlers passed this law that no woman should have right of inheritance in Salic land. And the Salic land—the region between the Elbe and the Sala, in Germany, as I said—is now called Meissen. It is clear, then, that

Then doth it well appear the Salic law
Was not devisèd for the realm of France,
Nor did the French possess the Salic land
Until four hundred one and twenty years
After defunction of King Pharamond,
Idly supposed the founder of this law;
Who died within the year of our redemption
Four hundred twenty-six; and Charles the Great
Subdued the Saxons and did seat the French
Beyond the river Sala in the year
Eight hundred five. Besides, their writers say,
King Pepin, which deposèd Childeric,
Did, as heir general, being descended
Of Blithild, which was daughter to King Clothair,
Make claim and title to the crown of France.
Hugh Capet also, who usurped the crown
Of Charles the duke of Lorraine, sole heir male
Of the true line and stock of Charles the Great,
To find his title with some shows of truth,
Though in pure truth it was corrupt and naught,
Conveyed himself as th' heir to th' Lady Lingare,
Daughter to Charlemagne, who was the son
To Lewis the Emperor, and Lewis the son
Of Charles the Great. Also King Lewis the Tenth,
Who was sole heir to the usurper Capet,
Could not keep quiet in his conscience,
Wearing the crown of France, till satisfied
That fair Queen Isabel, his grandmother,
Was lineal of the Lady Ermengare,
Daughter to Charles the foresaid duke of Lorraine,
By the which marriage the line of Charles the Great
Was reunited to the crown of France.
So that, as clear as is the summer's sun,
King Pepin's title and Hugh Capet's claim,
King Lewis his satisfaction, all appear
To hold in right and title of the female.

the Salic law was not intended for the realm of France. Nor did the French possess the Salic land until four hundred twenty-one years after the death of King Pharamond, incorrectly thought to be the founder of the law. He died in the year 426, and Charles the Great conquered the Saxons and settled Frenchmen in the region beyond the river Sala in the year 805. Besides, according to the French historians, King Pepin, who deposed Childeric, based his own claim to the crown of France on his descent from Blithild, the daughter of King Clothair. Another case: Hugh Capet, who usurped the crown from Charles the duke of Lorraine—sole male heir in a direct line from Charles the Great—passed himself off as heir to Lady Lingare, daughter of Charlemagne, who was the son of Lewis the Emperor (who was the son of Charles the Great), in order to give his claim to the throne more validity (though, in fact, the claim was completely false and worthless). Another case: King Lewis the Tenth, who was sole heir to the usurper Capet, could not rest easy as king until he was assured that Queen Isabel, his grandmother, was a direct descendent of the Lady Ermengare, daughter of the aforementioned Charles duke of Lorraine, by which marriage the line of Charles the Great was reunited with the throne of France. Thus, it should be clear as day that King Pepin's title, Hugh Capet's claim, and the resolution of King Lewis's doubts all plainly derive from the female.

So do the kings of France unto this day,
Howbeit they would hold up this Salic law
To bar your Highness claiming from the female
And rather choose to hide them in a net
Than amply to imbar their crooked titles
Usurped from you and your progenitors.

KING HENRY

May I with right and conscience make this claim?

CANTERBURY

The sin upon my head, dread sovereign,
For in the Book of Numbers is it writ:
"When the man dies, let the inheritance
Descend unto the daughter." Gracious lord,
Stand for your own, unwind your bloody flag,
Look back into your mighty ancestors.
Go, my dread lord, to your great-grandsire's tomb,
From whom you claim. Invoke his warlike spirit
And your great-uncle's, Edward the Black Prince,
Who on the French ground played a tragedy,
Making defeat on the full power of France
Whiles his most mighty father on a hill
Stood smiling to behold his lion's whelp
Forage in blood of French nobility.
O noble English, that could entertain
With half their forces the full pride of France
And let another half stand laughing by,
All out of work and cold for action!

ELY

Awake remembrance of these valiant dead
And with your puissant arm renew their feats.
You are their heir, you sit upon their throne,
The blood and courage that renownèd them
Runs in your veins; and my thrice-puissant liege
Is in the very May-morn of his youth,
Ripe for exploits and mighty enterprises.

To this day, the kings of France follow this unspoken rule, even though they point to this Salic law to bar your Highness from inheriting it through the female line. They prefer to obscure matters rather than reveal how corrupt their own claims to the French crown are. They usurped that crown from you and your ancestors.

KING HENRY

Can I justifiably and in good conscience make this claim?

CANTERBURY

If not, mighty sovereign, let the blame be mine. For it is written in the book of Numbers: "When the man dies, let the inheritance descend unto the daughter." Gracious lord, claim what is yours. Unfurl your banners of war. Take your mighty ancestors as models. Go to the tomb of your great-grandfather, from whom your own title to the crown derives. Invoke his warlike spirit and that of Edward the Black Prince, your great-uncle, who fought a tragic battle on French soil, routing the French army in full force while his mighty father stood by on a hilltop, smiling to see his son steeped in the blood of French noblemen. O noble English, who could take on the entire French army with only half their forces, leaving the other half to stand by, idle and laughing.

ELY

Awaken the memory of those valiant ancestors and with your own powerful arm make their deeds live again. You are their heir and sit on their throne, and the blood and courage that glorified them run in your veins. You, my most powerful sovereign, are in the very prime of youth, ripe for glorious deeds and great enterprises.

EXETER

Your brother kings and monarchs of the earth
Do all expect that you should rouse yourself
As did the former lions of your blood.

WESTMORELAND

They know your Grace hath cause and means and might;
So hath your Highness. Never king of England
Had nobles richer, and more loyal subjects,
Whose hearts have left their bodies here in England
And lie pavilioned in the fields of France.

CANTERBURY

Oh, let their bodies follow, my dear liege,
With blood and sword and fire to win your right,
In aid whereof we of the spiritualty
Will raise your Highness such a mighty sum
As never did the clergy at one time
Bring in to any of your ancestors.

KING HENRY

We must not only arm t' invade the French,
But lay down our proportions to defend
Against the Scot, who will make road upon us
With all advantages.

CANTERBURY

They of those marches, gracious sovereign,
Shall be a wall sufficient to defend
Our inland from the pilfering borderers.

KING HENRY

We do not mean the coursing snatchers only,
But fear the main intendment of the Scot,
Who hath been still a giddy neighbor to us.
For you shall read that my great-grandfather
Never went with his forces into France
But that the Scot on his unfurnished kingdom
Came pouring like the tide into a breach
With ample and brim fullness of his force,
Galling the gleanèd land with hot assays,

EXETER

The other kings throughout the world all expect you to take the offensive, just like your lion-hearted forebears.

WESTMORELAND

They know your Grace has justification, as well as the money and military strength. And so you do. No king of England was ever backed by wealthier nobles or more loyal subjects. Their bodies may remain here in England, but their hearts are encamped on the fields of France already.

CANTERBURY

Oh, let their bodies follow, my dear king, to win back what's rightfully yours with blood and sword and fire. And to that end, we, the clergy, will raise your Highness a sum greater than your ancestors were ever given at any one time.

KING HENRY

We must not only arm ourselves to invade France, but must also apportion troops to defend against invasion by the Scots, who will see this as a perfect opportunity to attack.

CANTERBURY

Your subjects in the north, gracious sovereign, will provide a wall of defense against Scottish thieves across the border.

KING HENRY

I don't mean merely bands of thieves. What we have to worry about is a full-scale invasion from Scotland—always an unreliable neighbor. You'll find that my great-grandfather never went to war with France without Scotland making an attack on his undefended kingdom, pouring in full force like the tide through a gap in a dyke, troubling the depleted country with violent attacks, and laying siege to towns and castles.

Girding with grievous siege castles and towns,
That England, being empty of defense,
Hath shook and trembled at th' ill neighborhood.

CANTERBURY

She hath been then more feared than harmed, my liege,
For hear her but exampled by herself:
When all her chivalry hath been in France
And she a mourning widow of her nobles,
She hath herself not only well defended
But taken and impounded as a stray
The king of Scots, whom she did send to France
To fill King Edward's fame with prisoner kings
And make her chronicle as rich with praise
As is the ooze and bottom of the sea
With sunken wrack and sumless treasuries.

ELY

But there's a saying very old and true:
"If that you will France win,
Then with Scotland first begin."
For once the eagle England being in prey,
To her unguarded nest the weasel Scot
Comes sneaking and so sucks her princely eggs,
Playing the mouse in absence of the cat,
To 'tame and havoc more than she can eat.

EXETER

It follows, then, the cat must stay at home.
Yet that is but a crushed necessity,
Since we have locks to safeguard necessaries
And pretty traps to catch the petty thieves.
While that the armèd hand doth fight abroad,
Th' advisèd head defends itself at home.
For government, though high and low and lower,
Put into parts, doth keep in one consent,
Congreeing in a full and natural close,
Like music.

The whole of England, being unprotected, trembled with fear.

CANTERBURY

But the country was more frightened than hurt, my liege. Take this example: when all its knights have been in France and all its noblemen absent, England has not only defended itself well, but actually seized the Scottish king and penned him up like a stray dog. Then he was sent off to France. He enhanced King Edward's fame, adding royalty to his captives and thus making England's own history as rich with glory as the muddy floor of the sea is rich with sunken ships and innumerable treasures.

ELY

But here's an old, true saying: "If you want to win France, start with Scotland." For when the eagle England leaves her nest to seek prey, the weasel Scot always comes sneaking around to suck dry her princely eggs and, like the mouse when the cat's away, destroy more than she can actually eat.

EXETER

It would follow from this that the cat should stay home. But that is a false conclusion, since we have locks to keep our valuables safe and clever traps to catch little thieves. While the armed hand fights in foreign lands, the wise head defends itself at home. For though the state is divided into different levels and functions, it all works in agreement for a unified purpose, a natural and perfect end such as we find in music.

CANTERBURY

Therefore doth heaven divide
The state of man in diverse functions,
Setting endeavor in continual motion,
To which is fixèd as an aim or butt
Obedience; for so work the honeybees,
Creatures that by a rule in nature teach
The act of order to a peopled kingdom.
They have a king and officers of sorts,
Where some like magistrates correct at home,
Others like merchants venture trade abroad,
Others like soldiers armèd in their stings
Make boot upon the summer's velvet buds,
Which pillage they with merry march bring home
To the tent royal of their emperor,
Who, busied in his majesty, surveys
The singing masons building roofs of gold,
The civil citizens kneading up the honey,
The poor mechanic porters crowding in
Their heavy burdens at his narrow gate,
The sad-eyed justice with his surly hum
Delivering o'er to executors pale
The lazy yawning drone. I this infer:
That many things, having full reference
To one consent, may work contrariously,
As many arrows loosèd several ways
Come to one mark, as many ways meet in one town,
As many fresh streams meet in one salt sea,
As many lines close in the dial's center,
So may a thousand actions, once afoot,
End in one purpose, and be all well borne
Without defeat. Therefore to France, my liege!
Divide your happy England into four,
Whereof take you one quarter into France,
And you withal shall make all Gallia shake.

CANTERBURY

That is why God divided humanity into various functions, so as to keep human endeavor moving ever forward, the one single fixed element—the aim—being obedience. Honey bees operate in just such a communal way. In fact, you can learn a lot about how to run a well-ordered kingdom from these creatures. They have a king and officers of sorts. Some, like magistrates, dole out punishment at home, while others venture forth for commerce, like merchants. Still others, armed like soldiers with stingers, pillage the summer flowers, bringing the booty triumphantly home to the royal tent of their emperor, who is preoccupied with governing. The emperor supervises the masons as they build gold roofs, the ordinary citizens as they process the honey, the humble laborers as they crowd through the city's narrow gate with their heavy burdens, and the solemn-looking judge (with his grouchy hum) as he delivers lazy, unproductive drones to pale executioners. From this, I conclude that many different elements can work toward one common end—just as many arrows, shot from different points, converge on a single target; just as many roads meet in a single town; just as many fresh streams empty into only one salt sea; just as the many radiuses of a sundial unite at its center. Just so, a thousand actions, once set in motion, will result in one desired object, and all will be well carried out and have a successful end. Therefore, head to France, my liege! Divide your lucky England into four. If you take even one quarter with you to France, you will nevertheless make the whole country shake.

A sundial is a device that tells time, with a straight edge casting a shadow on a flat metal plate.

If we, with thrice such powers left at home,
Cannot defend our own doors from the dog,
Let us be worried, and our nation lose
The name of hardiness and policy.

KING HENRY
Call in the messengers sent from the Dauphin.

Exeunt some attendants

Now are we well resolved, and by God's help
And yours, the noble sinews of our power,
France being ours, we'll bend it to our awe
Or break it all to pieces. Or there we'll sit,
Ruling in large and ample empery
O'er France and all her almost kingly dukedoms,
Or lay these bones in an unworthy urn,
Tombless, with no remembrance over them.
Either our history shall with full mouth
Speak freely of our acts, or else our grave,
Like Turkish mute, shall have a tongueless mouth,
Not worshipped with a waxen epitaph.

Enter AMBASSADORS *of France, with attendants*

Now are we well prepared to know the pleasure
Of our fair cousin Dauphin, for we hear
Your greeting is from him, not from the king.

AMBASSADOR
May 't please your Majesty to give us leave
Freely to render what we have in charge,
Or shall we sparingly show you far off
The Dauphin's meaning and our embassy?

If we cannot defend our country with three times such a power left at home, then we deserve to be harassed by an invader and lose our reputation as a powerful and politically savvy nation.

KING HENRY
Call in the messengers sent from the Dauphin.

Some attendants exit.

Now I've made up my mind, and with God's help—and yours, you nobles who are the mainstay of my power—I'll force France to fear me, or I'll break her into pieces, as she's rightfully mine. Either I'll sit, ruling with absolute authority over France and all her dukedoms, or I'll lay these bones in a common grave, with no stone or inscription over them. Either the story of my deeds will be declaimed loudly and without restraint, or else my grave will remain speechless, like a Turkish mute, not honored with even an epitaph etched in wax.

French AMBASSADORS *enter.*

I'm ready now to hear what my good cousin the Dauphin has to say—for I hear that the greeting you bear is from him, not the king.

FIRST AMBASSADOR
Will your Majesty grant us permission to freely express the message we've been asked to convey? Or should we be tactful and only hint at what the Dauphin sent us to say?

KING HENRY

We are no tyrant, but a Christian king,
Unto whose grace our passion is as subject
As is our wretches fettered in our prisons.
Therefore with frank and with uncurbèd plainness
Tell us the Dauphin's mind.

AMBASSADOR

Thus, then, in few:
Your Highness, lately sending into France,
Did claim some certain dukedoms in the right
Of your great predecessor, King Edward the Third;
In answer of which claim, the prince our master
Says that you savor too much of your youth
And bids you be advised there's naught in France
That can be with a nimble galliard won.
You cannot revel into dukedoms there.
He therefore sends you, meeter for your spirit,
This tun of treasure, and, in lieu of this,
Desires you let the dukedoms that you claim
Hear no more of you. This the Dauphin speaks.

KING HENRY

What treasure, uncle?

EXETER

Tennis balls, my liege.

KING HENRY

—Convey them with safe conduct.—Fare you well. We are
glad the Dauphin is so pleasant with us.
His present and your pains we thank you for.
When we have matched our rackets to these balls,
We will in France, by God's grace, play a set
Shall strike his father's crown into the hazard.
Tell him he hath made a match with such a wrangler
That all the courts of France will be disturbed
With chases. And we understand him well,
How he comes o'er us with our wilder days,
Not measuring what use we made of them.

KING HENRY

I am no tyrant but a Christian king, whose emotions are as tightly controlled as the wretches who languish in our prisons. Therefore tell me the Dauphin's mind frankly and without constraint.

FIRST AMBASSADOR

Here it is then, in as few words as possible. Your Highness recently sent word to France claiming certain dukedoms as your own, in the name of your great ancestor, King Edward the Third. By way of answer, the prince our master says that you're acting like the immature youth that you are. He warns you to take note: there's nothing in France that you can win by dancing. You can't party your way into dukedoms there. He therefore sends you this casket of treasure as a gift more suited to your character. And in return for this gift, he wishes you to drop your claim to the dukedoms. This is the Dauphin's message.

KING HENRY

What's the treasure, uncle?

EXETER

Tennis balls, my liege.

KING HENRY

I'm happy the Dauphin has such a good sense of humor. Thank you for his present and your trouble. Once I've put my rackets to these balls, I'll play a set in France, God willing, that will knock his father's crown right out of the court. Tell him he's got himself such a willing opponent that we'll be chasing balls all over France. And I understand perfectly his sneering reference to my wilder days. He doesn't realize how useful they were to me. For a long time, I didn't value this humble throne of England, and therefore lived at some remove and gave myself over to riotous living.

We never valued this poor seat of England
And therefore, living hence, did give ourself
To barbarous license, as 'tis ever common
That men are merriest when they are from home.
But tell the Dauphin I will keep my state,
Be like a king, and show my sail of greatness
When I do rouse me in my throne of France,
For that I have laid by my majesty
And plodded like a man for working days.
But I will rise there with so full a glory
That I will dazzle all the eyes of France,
Yea, strike the Dauphin blind to look on us.
And tell the pleasant prince this mock of his
Hath turned his balls to gun-stones, and his soul
Shall stand sore chargèd for the wasteful vengeance
That shall fly with them; for many a thousand widows
Shall this his mock mock out of their dear husbands,
Mock mothers from their sons, mock castles down,
And some are yet ungotten and unborn
That shall have cause to curse the Dauphin's scorn.
But this lies all within the will of God,
To whom I do appeal, and in whose name
Tell you the Dauphin I am coming on,
To venge me as I may and to put forth
My rightful hand in a well-hallowed cause.
So get you hence in peace. And tell the Dauphin
His jest will savor but of shallow wit
When thousands weep more than did laugh at it.

Exeunt AMBASSADORS, *with attendants*

EXETER
This was a merry message.

Men tend to be at their most irresponsible when they're away from home. But tell the Dauphin I will retain the dignity of kingship and appear all the more royal and glorious on the throne of France. Precisely for this purpose I went about like a commoner and experienced the life of the ordinary man. Now I'll rise there with such glory that I'll dazzle all the eyes of France. I'll shine so brightly that even the Dauphin will be struck blind. And tell the laughing prince that this joke of his has transformed his tennis balls into cannon balls, and the destructive vengeance they bring with them will be his responsibility. His mocking will mock many thousands of widows out of their husbands. It will mock mothers out of their sons, and mock castles down. There are people yet unborn and unconceived who will have reason to curse the Dauphin's scorn. But all this lies with God, to whom I do appeal. In God's name, inform the Dauphin I am coming, to avenge myself and to put forth my rightful hand in a sanctified cause. So go in peace. And tell the Dauphin his joke will look pretty stupid when thousands more weep than ever laughed at it. *(to attendants)* Give them safe conduct.—Farewell.

The **AMBASSADORS** *exit, with some attendants.*

EXETER

That was a humorous message.

KING HENRY

We hope to make the sender blush at it.
Therefore, my lords, omit no happy hour
That may give furth'rance to our expedition;
For we have now no thought in us but France,
Save those to God, that run before our business.
Therefore let our proportions for these wars
Be soon collected, and all things thought upon
That may with reasonable swiftness add
More feathers to our wings. For, God before,
We'll chide this Dauphin at his father's door.
Therefore let every man now task his thought,
That this fair action may on foot be brought.

Flourish

Exeunt

KING HENRY

I hope to make the sender blush for it. Now, lords, don't let slip any opportunity that might be advantageous for our expedition. My thoughts are now bent entirely on France—except my thoughts about God, who takes precedence over this undertaking. Therefore, let's set about mustering the requisite number of troops and give consideration to anything that can be expected to speed our enterprise. For, with God on our side, we'll chastise this prince on his father's own doorstep. Therefore, let every man give some thought to how this noble expedition may be undertaken.

Trumpets sound.

They all exit.

ACT TWO

PROLOGUE

Enter CHORUS

CHORUS

Now all the youth of England are on fire,
And silken dalliance in the wardrobe lies.
Now thrive the armorers, and honor's thought
Reigns solely in the breast of every man.
They sell the pasture now to buy the horse,
Following the mirror of all Christian kings
With wingèd heels, as English Mercurys.
For now sits Expectation in the air
And hides a sword, from hilts unto the point,
With crowns imperial, crowns and coronets
Promised to Harry and his followers.
The French, advised by good intelligence
Of this most dreadful preparation,
Shake in their fear, and with pale policy
Seek to divert the English purposes.
O England, model to thy inward greatness,
Like little body with a mighty heart,
What might'st thou do, that honor would thee do,
Were all thy children kind and natural!
But see, thy fault France hath in thee found out,
A nest of hollow bosoms, which he fills
With treacherous crowns, and three corrupted men—
One, Richard, Earl of Cambridge, and the second,
Henry, Lord Scroop of Masham, and the third,
Sir Thomas Grey, knight, of Northumberland—
Have, for the gilt of France (Oh, guilt indeed!),
Confirmed conspiracy with fearful France,
And by their hands this grace of kings must die,
If hell and treason hold their promises,

ACT TWO

PROLOGUE

The CHORUS *enters.*

CHORUS

Now all the young men of England are inspired and have stored their party clothes in the closet. Armorers are doing great business, and all men think about is honor. People are selling off their land to buy warhorses so they can follow the exemplary king into battle as if they had winged feet, like Mercury. There's a sense of anticipation in the air. In the minds of Harry and his followers, visions of the kingdoms, spoils, and titles to be won eclipse thoughts of actual fighting. The French, meanwhile, have been forewarned of all this preparation by their spies and tremble in fear. They seek to derail the English with cowardly tricks. Oh, England! You are physically small but inwardly great, like a mighty heart enclosed in a small body. There is nothing you couldn't accomplish if all your subjects were loyal and loving! But, see, the king of France has detected your weak spot: a nest of faithless traitors, whose treachery he has purchased with gold. Three corrupt men—Richard, earl of Cambridge; Henry, Lord Scroop of Masham; and Sir Thomas Grey, knight, of Northumberland—have agreed to conspire with the French in exchange for money. The gracious king will die by their hands in Southampton before he sets sail for France—if Hell and treason have their way. Stick with us, ladies and gentlemen, and we'll make a play, conquering space and time. Imagine that the traitors have been paid and made their choice. The king has left London, and the scene now

In Roman mythology, Mercury is the messenger of the gods, often depicted with winged feet.

Ere he take ship for France, and in Southampton.
Linger your patience on, and we'll digest
Th' abuse of distance, force a play.
The sum is paid, the traitors are agreed,
The king is set from London, and the scene
Is now transported, gentles, to Southampton.
There is the playhouse now, there must you sit,
And thence to France shall we convey you safe
And bring you back, charming the narrow seas
To give you gentle pass; for, if we may,
We'll not offend one stomach with our play.
But, till the king come forth, and not till then,
Unto Southampton do we shift our scene.

Exit

shifts, friends, to Southampton. That's where you must pretend the theater is; that's where you must sit. From there we'll safely carry you to France and back, calming the waters of the Channel to provide you with a smooth voyage. For if we can help it, we'd just as soon nobody was made sick by our play. But we won't shift the scene to Southampton until Henry reappears.

The CHORUS *exits.*

ACT 2, SCENE 1

Enter Corporal NYM *and Lieutenant* BARDOLPH

BARDOLPH
Well met, Corporal Nym.

NYM
Good morrow, Lieutenant Bardolph.

BARDOLPH
What, are Ancient Pistol and you friends yet?

NYM
For my part, I care not. I say little, but when time shall serve, there shall be smiles; but that shall be as it may. I dare not fight, but I will wink and hold out mine iron. It is a simple one, but what though? It will toast cheese, and it will endure cold as another man's sword will, and there's an end.

BARDOLPH
I will bestow a breakfast to make you friends; and we'll be all three sworn brothers to France. Let 't be so, good Corporal Nym.

NYM
Faith, I will live so long as I may, that's the certain of it. And when I cannot live any longer, I will do as I may. That is my rest; that is the rendezvous of it.

BARDOLPH
It is certain, corporal, that he is married to Nell Quickly, and certainly she did you wrong, for you were troth-plight to her.

NYM
I cannot tell. Things must be as they may. Men may sleep, and they may have their throats about them at that time, and some say knives have edges. It must be as it may.

ACT 2, SCENE 1

Corporal NYM *and Lieutenant* BARDOLPH *enter.*

BARDOLPH
Good to see you, Corporal Nym.

NYM
Good day, Lieutenant Bardolph.

BARDOLPH
Tell me, are you and Ensign Pistol friends again yet?

NYM
For my part, I really don't care. I don't say much, but when the time comes, we'll smile at each other. But that's as it may be. I won't fight, but I can close my eyes and take a swipe with my sword—just a simple sword, but so what? It's good enough to toast cheese, and it will survive cold as well as another man's sword. And that's that.

BARDOLPH
I'll buy you both breakfast if it will make you two friends. Then we can all three be comrades on our way to France. How about it, Corporal Nym?

NYM
Well, I will live until I die, that's for sure, and when I can't live anymore, I'll deal with it. That's it. That's really all I can say.

BARDOLPH
It's true, corporal, that he is married to Nell Quickly. And it's true that she did you wrong, since you were engaged to her.

NYM
It's not for me to say. Things are what they are. Men may sleep, and when they do they may have their throats with them, and some people say knives have blades. What must be must be, and though my

Though patience be a tired mare, yet she will plod. There must be conclusions. Well, I cannot tell.

Enter PISTOL *and* HOSTESS

BARDOLPH

Here comes Ancient Pistol and his wife. Good corporal, be patient here.—How now, mine host Pistol?

PISTOL

Base tyke, call'st thou me host?
Now, by this hand, I swear, I scorn the term,
Nor shall my Nell keep lodgers.

HOSTESS

No, by my troth, not long, for we cannot lodge and board a dozen or fourteen gentlewomen that live honestly by the prick of their needles but it will be thought we keep a bawdy house straight.

NYM *and* PISTOL *draw*

Oh, well-a-day, Lady! If he be not hewn now, we shall see willful adultery and murder committed.

BARDOLPH

Good lieutenant, good corporal, offer nothing here.

NYM

Pish!

PISTOL

Pish for thee, Iceland dog,
Thou prick-eared cur of Iceland!

HOSTESS

Good Corporal Nym, show thy valor and put up your sword.

NYM

Will you shog off? *(to* PISTOL*)* I would have you *solus.*

patience is worn out, it will last a little longer. There must be some resolution. Well, it's not for me to say.

PISTOL *and* **HOSTESS QUICKLY** *enter.*

BARDOLPH

Here comes Ensign Pistol and his wife. Be cool now, corporal.—How are you, Pistol, my good host?

PISTOL

You peasant dog, are you calling me a host? I swear, I scorn the word. My Nell isn't going to be taking any lodgers.

HOSTESS QUICKLY

No, not for long, that's certain. For we couldn't even put up a dozen or so nice girls who make an honest living sewing without our neighbors thinking we were running a brothel.

NYM *and* **PISTOL** *draw their swords.*

Oh, dear. If he isn't cut down in his tracks right now, we'll see willful adultery and murder committed. Good lieutenant, good corporal, don't fight each other here.

"Willful adultery and murder" is an example of the humorous nonsense Mistress Quickly speaks.

NYM

Pish!

PISTOL

Pish to you, you mangy dog, you pointy-eared Icelandic mutt.

HOSTESS QUICKLY

Corporal Nym, be a man and put away your sword.

NYM

Get lost, will you? (*to* **PISTOL**) I'd like to get you *solus*.

Solus means "alone" in Latin.

PISTOL

"Solus," egregious dog? O viper vile,
The *solus* in thy most marvelous face,
The *solus* in thy teeth and in thy throat
And in thy hateful lungs, yea, in thy maw, perdy,
And, which is worse, within thy nasty mouth!
I do retort the *solus* in thy bowels,
For I can take, and Pistol's cock is up,
And flashing fire will follow.

NYM

I am not Barbason; you cannot conjure me. I have an humor to knock you indifferently well. If you grow foul with me, Pistol, I will scour you with my rapier, as I may, in fair terms. If you would walk off, I would prick your guts a little in good terms, as I may, and that's the humor of it.

PISTOL

O braggart vile and damnèd furious wight,
The grave doth gape, and doting death is near.
Therefore exhale.

BARDOLPH

Hear me, hear me what I say: he that strikes the first stroke, I'll run him up to the hilts, as I am a soldier. *(draws)*

PISTOL

An oath of mickle might, and fury shall abate.
Give me thy fist, thy forefoot to me give.
Thy spirits are most tall.

NYM

I will cut thy throat one time or other in fair terms, that is the humor of it.

PISTOL

Couple à gorge, that is the word. I defy thee again.
O hound of Crete, think'st thou my spouse to get?
No, to the spital go,
And from the powd'ring tub of infamy
Fetch forth the lazar kite of Cressid's kind,
Doll Tearsheet she by name, and her espouse.

PISTOL

Solus, you unspeakable dog? You loathsome snake, I throw your *solus* in that weird face of yours, in your teeth and your throat and in your hateful lungs, and even worse, in your nasty mouth! Shove that *solus* into your bowels, because I can take you. My gun is cocked and ready to fire.

NYM

I am not some fiend of hell: you can't get rid of me with spells. I'm in a mood to beat you up pretty good. If you get nasty with me, Pistol, I'll stab you with my sword, in fair play. If you'd like to step aside with me, I'll give you a little prick in the guts, all in fair play, if I can, and that's the way it is.

PISTOL

You revolting braggart and hellish creature! Your grave is gaping open, and your death is near. So take your last breath.

BARDOLPH

Listen, listen to what I say: whoever strikes first, I'll run him through with my sword, as sure as I'm a soldier. *(drawing his sword)*

PISTOL

That's an oath of great power, and our fury must subside. *(PISTOL and NYM sheath their swords)* Give me your hand—your forefoot. You have a brave spirit.

NYM

I'll cut your throat, sooner or later—that's just how it is.

PISTOL

"Couple à gorge" is corrupt French for "cut the throat."

Couple à gorge is the word for what you're trying to say. I defy you again. You dog, do you think you'll take my wife? No, go to the hospital, into the ward where they treat venereal disease, and get yourself a leprous, diseased prostitute like Doll Tearsheet and marry her.

I have, and I will hold, the quondam Quickly
For the only she, And—*pauca*—there's enough. Go to.

Enter the BOY

BOY

Mine host Pistol, you must come to my master and your hostess. He is very sick and would to bed.—Good Bardolph, put thy face between his sheets, and do the office of a warming-pan. Faith, he's very ill.

BARDOLPH

Away, you rogue!

HOSTESS

By my troth, he'll yield the crow a pudding one of these days. The king has killed his heart. Good husband, come home presently.

Exeunt HOSTESS *and* BOY

BARDOLPH

Come, shall I make you two friends? We must to France together. Why the devil should we keep knives to cut one another's throats?

PISTOL

Let floods o'erswell and fiends for food howl on!

NYM

You'll pay me the eight shillings I won of you at betting?

PISTOL

Base is the slave that pays.

NYM

That now I will have—that's the humor of it.

PISTOL

As manhood shall compound. Push home.

I won the former Mistress Quickly and I'll keep her as my only wife, and—Damn it! That's enough. Come on!

A BOY *enters.*

BOY

My host Pistol, you must come to my master. You too, my hostess: he is very sick and should be put to bed. Bardolph, put your face between his sheets and act as a warming pan. Really, he's very sick!

In Shakespeare's Henry IV plays, Bardolph's face is described as flaming red with acne.

BARDOLPH

Get out of here, you punk!

HOSTESS QUICKLY

I swear, he'll be food for the crows soon. The king has broken his heart. Good husband, come home soon.

HOSTESS QUICKLY *and* BOY *exit.*

BARDOLPH

Come on, can I get you two to make up? We have to go to France together: why should we cut each other's throats?

PISTOL

Let rivers flood and fiends howl for food!

NYM

Are you going to pay the eight shillings I won from you in a bet?

PISTOL

Paying debts is for peasants.

NYM

I'm going to take it from you now. That's how it is.

PISTOL

We'll see, won't we? Do your best.

They draw

BARDOLPH
By this sword, he that makes the first thrust, I'll kill him. By this sword, I will.

PISTOL
"Sword" is an oath, and oaths must have their course.

BARDOLPH
Corporal Nym, an thou wilt be friends, be friends; an thou wilt not, why then be enemies with me too. Prithee, put up.

PISTOL
A noble shalt thou have, and present pay,
And liquor likewise will I give to thee,
And friendship shall combine, and brotherhood.
I'll live by Nym, and Nym shall live by me.
Is not this just? For I shall subtler be
Unto the camp, and profits will accrue.
Give me thy hand.

NYM
I shall have my noble?

PISTOL
In cash, most justly paid.

NYM
Well, then, that's the humor of 't.

Enter HOSTESS

HOSTESS
As ever you come of women, come in quickly to Sir John. Ah, poor heart, he is so shaked of a burning quotidian-tertian that it is most lamentable to behold. Sweet men, come to him.

NYM
The king hath run bad humors on the knight, that's the even of it.

They draw their swords.

BARDOLPH

By this sword, I'll kill whichever one of you makes the first thrust. By this sword, I will.

PISTOL

"By this sword" is an oath, and oaths must be kept.

BARDOLPH

Corporal Nym, if you want to be friends, be friends. If not, then you can be my enemy, too. Come on, put it away.

PISTOL

A noble is a coin worth slightly less than the eight shillings he owes Nym.

I'll give you a noble right now, and I'll give you liquor, too, and friendship and brotherhood. I'll live for Nym, and Nym will live for me. Is that fair? For I'll be selling provisions to the troops, and there'll be profits to go around. Give me your hand.

NYM

I'll get my noble?

PISTOL

In cash.

NYM

Well, then, that's how it is.

HOSTESS QUICKLY *enters.*

HOSTESS QUICKLY

If you ever had a mother, come in quickly to Sir John. The poor thing, he is so shaken with a fever that it's terrible to see. Sweet men, come to him.

NYM

The king has done him a bad turn. That's all there is to it.

PISTOL

Nym, thou hast spoke the right.
His heart is fracted and corroborate.

NYM

The king is a good king, but it must be as it may. He passes some humors and careers.

PISTOL

Let us condole the knight, for, lambkins, we will live.

Exeunt

PISTOL

Nym, what you say is true. His heart is broken and corroborate.

"Corroborate" means "strengthened" or "confirmed" and is probably not what Pistol means

NYM

The king is a good king, but things must be as they may. He has his moods and his ways.

PISTOL

Let us go sit with the knight; for, my little lambs, we will survive him.

They all exit.

ACT 2, SCENE 2

Enter EXETER, BEDFORD, *and* WESTMORELAND

BEDFORD
'Fore God, his grace is bold to trust these traitors.

EXETER
They shall be apprehended by and by.

WESTMORELAND
How smooth and even they do bear themselves,
As if allegiance in their bosoms sat
Crownèd with faith and constant loyalty.

BEDFORD
The king hath note of all that they intend,
By interception which they dream not of.

EXETER
Nay, but the man that was his bedfellow,
Whom he hath dulled and cloyed with gracious favors—
That he should, for a foreign purse, so sell
His sovereign's life to death and treachery!

Trumpets sound. Enter KING HENRY, SCROOP, CAMBRIDGE, GREY, *and attendants*

KING HENRY
Now sits the wind fair, and we will aboard.
—My Lord of Cambridge, and my kind Lord of Masham,
And you, my gentle knight, give me your thoughts.
Think you not that the powers we bear with us
Will cut their passage through the force of France,
Doing the execution and the act
For which we have in head assembled them?

SCROOP
No doubt, my liege, if each man do his best.

ACT 2, SCENE 2

EXETER, **BEDFORD**, *and* **WESTMORELAND** *enter.*

BEDFORD

I must say, the king is taking a bold risk letting these traitors go free.

EXETER

They'll be arrested in a little while.

WESTMORELAND

How smooth and cool they seem! Just as if they were perfectly loyal and faithful.

BEDFORD

The king has been informed of all their plans, but they have no idea.

EXETER

No, but it's unbelievable that the man who was his dearest friend, a man he has showered with love and favor, would repay the king with treachery, selling his own sovereign's life to a foreign power!

Trumpets sound. **KING HENRY**, **SCROOP**, **CAMBRIDGE**, *and* **GREY** *enter, with attendants.*

KING HENRY

Now that the wind is favorable, let's board the ship. —My Lord of Cambridge and my good Lord of Masham and you, my noble knight, what do you think? Will our army cut a swath through the fighting force of France, achieving and accomplishing everything I've assembled them to do?

SCROOP

No doubt it will, my liege, if each man does his best.

KING HENRY

I doubt not that, since we are well-persuaded
We carry not a heart with us from hence
That grows not in a fair consent with ours,
Nor leave not one behind that doth not wish
Success and conquest to attend on us.

CAMBRIDGE

Never was monarch better feared and loved
Than is your Majesty. There's not, I think, a subject
That sits in heart-grief and uneasiness
Under the sweet shade of your government.

GREY

True. Those that were your father's enemies
Have steeped their galls in honey, and do serve you
With hearts create of duty and of zeal.

KING HENRY

We therefore have great cause of thankfulness
And shall forget the office of our hand
Sooner than quittance of desert and merit
According to the weight and worthiness.

SCROOP

So service shall with steelèd sinews toil,
And labor shall refresh itself with hope
To do your Grace incessant services.

KING HENRY

We judge no less.—Uncle of Exeter,
Enlarge the man committed yesterday
That railed against our person. We consider
it was excess of wine that set him on,
And on his more advice we pardon him.

SCROOP

That's mercy, but too much security.
Let him be punished, sovereign, lest example
Breed, by his sufferance, more of such a kind.

KING HENRY

Oh, let us yet be merciful.

KING HENRY

I have no doubt about that, since I know there isn't a man among us who isn't with me wholeheartedly, or a soul left behind who doesn't wish us success and conquest.

CAMBRIDGE

There never was a monarch better feared and loved than yourself, your Majesty. I don't think there's a single unhappy subject living under the protection of your government.

GREY

True. Those who were bitter enemies of your father in his time have turned their bitterness to sweetness, serving you loyally and wholeheartedly.

KING HENRY

Yes, I have great cause to be thankful. I'm more likely to forget how to use my own hand than how to reward virtue and merit as they deserve.

SCROOP

And so your subjects serve you all the more energetically, hopeful of success and reward.

KING HENRY

I expect no less. Uncle of Exeter, release the man who was arrested yesterday for railing against me. I believe he only did it because he drank too much, and now that he's had a chance to think about his actions, I can pardon him.

SCROOP

That's merciful but a bit careless. He should be punished, your Majesty. If we tolerate such behavior, we're in danger of encouraging it.

KING HENRY

Oh, let us be merciful anyway.

CAMBRIDGE
So may Your Highness, and yet punish, too.

GREY
Sir, you show great mercy if you give him life
After the taste of much correction.

KING HENRY
Alas, your too much love and care of me
Are heavy orisons 'gainst this poor wretch.
If little faults proceeding on distemper
Shall not be winked at, how shall we stretch our eye
When capital crimes, chewed, swallowed, and digested,
Appear before us? We'll yet enlarge that man,
Though Cambridge, Scroop, and Grey, in their dear care
And tender preservation of our person,
Would have him punished. And now to our French causes.
Who are the late commissioners?

CAMBRIDGE
I one, my lord.
Your Highness bade me ask for it today.

SCROOP
So did you me, my liege.

GREY
And I, my royal sovereign.

KING HENRY
Then, Richard, Earl of Cambridge, there is yours.
—There yours, Lord Scroop of Masham.
—And, sir knight, Grey of Northumberland, this same
is yours. *(gives each of them a paper)*
—Read them, and know I know your worthiness.
—My Lord of Westmoreland and uncle Exeter,
We will aboard tonight.—Why, how now, gentlemen?
What see you in those papers, that you lose
So much complexion?—Look you, how they change.
Their cheeks are paper.—Why, what read you there
That have so cowarded and chased your blood
Out of appearance?

CAMBRIDGE

Your Highness could be merciful but still punish.

GREY

Sir, it would be merciful to let him live *after* beating him severely.

KING HENRY

I'm afraid your great love and concern for me lead you to deal too harshly with this poor fellow. If minor lapses caused by drunkenness are not to be tolerated, how will we punish capital crimes that result from much planning and forethought? No, I'll have that man released, despite the fact that Cambridge, Scroop, and Grey, in their extreme concern for my safety, would prefer that he were punished. And now, let's turn to our business with the French. Who are the new commissioners?

CAMBRIDGE

I am one, my lord. Your Highness told me to ask for my commission today.

SCROOP

You told me to do the same, my liege.

GREY

And me, too, my royal sovereign.

KING HENRY

In that case, there is yours, Richard Earl of Cambridge; there yours, Lord Scroop of Masham; and, sir knight, Grey of Northumberland, this one is yours. *(he gives each of them a piece of paper)* Read them, and trust that I recognize your true worth. My Lord of Westmoreland, and uncle Exeter, we will set sail night.—Why, what's this, gentlemen! What's in those papers that makes you change color?—Look how pale they're turning! Their cheeks are like paper.—What are you reading that makes you turn white?

CAMBRIDGE
I do confess my fault,
And do submit me to Your Highness' mercy.

GREY, SCROOP
To which we all appeal.

KING HENRY
The mercy that was quick in us but late
By your own counsel is suppressed and killed.
You must not dare, for shame, to talk of mercy,
For your own reasons turn into your bosoms,
As dogs upon their masters, worrying you.
—See you, my princes and my noble peers,
These English monsters. My Lord of Cambridge here,
You know how apt our love was to accord
To furnish him with all appurtenants
Belonging to his honor, and this man
Hath, for a few light crowns, lightly conspired,
And sworn unto the practices of France,
To kill us here in Hampton; to the which
This knight, no less for bounty bound to us
Than Cambridge is, hath likewise sworn.—But Oh,
What shall I say to thee, Lord Scroop, thou cruel,
Ingrateful, savage, and inhuman creature?
Thou that didst bear the key of all my counsels,
That knew'st the very bottom of my soul,
That almost mightst have coined me into gold,
Wouldst thou have practiced on me for thy use—
May it be possible that foreign hire
Could out of thee extract one spark of evil
That might annoy my finger? 'Tis so strange
That, though the truth of it stands off as gross
As black and white, my eye will scarcely see it.
Treason and murder ever kept together
As two yoke-devils sworn to either's purpose,
Working so grossly in a natural cause
That admiration did not whoop at them.

CAMBRIDGE

I confess my crime and throw myself on your Highness's mercy.

GREY AND SCROOP

To which we all appeal.

KING HENRY

The mercy that was alive in me a moment ago was smothered and killed by your own advice. For shame, don't talk of mercy. Your own arguments turn against you, like dogs who bite their own masters.—Princes and noble peers, take a look at these English monsters. Cambridge here, you know how I favored him and treated him with every respect due his rank. He was bought for a few coins, entering easily into this conspiracy with the French, promising to kill me here in Southhampton. And this knight, whom I've treated as generously as I have Cambridge, also joined the plot. But, oh, what can I say to you, Lord Scroop? You cruel, ungrateful, savage, and inhuman creature! You who had access to all my thoughts, who knew me to the inmost part of my soul, who could have had any amount of gold from me if you'd needed it and only asked me: is it possible that a foreign power could find in you even enough evil to injure one of my fingers? Though the truth of your treachery is as plain as black on white, I can scarcely believe it, it's so past understanding. Treason and murder have always gone together, like two devils joined in a common purpose. That's natural. But you, against all reason, added something new to the equation. You added the sheer improbability that you could do this. Whatever fiend it was that seduced you must win the prize for excellence in hell. All other devils who tempt people to treason patch together some motive, put together

But thou, 'gainst all proportion, didst bring in
Wonder to wait on treason and on murder,
And whatsoever cunning fiend it was
That wrought upon thee so preposterously
Hath got the voice in hell for excellence.
All other devils that suggest by treasons
Do botch and bungle up damnation
With patches, colors, and with forms being fetched
From glist'ring semblances of piety.
But he that tempered thee bade thee stand up,
Gave thee no instance why thou shouldst do treason,
Unless to dub thee with the name of traitor.
If that same demon that hath gulled thee thus
Should with his lion gait walk the whole world,
He might return to vasty Tartar back
And tell the legions "I can never win
A soul so easy as that Englishman's."
Oh, how hast thou with jealousy infected
The sweetness of affiance! Show men dutiful?
Why, so didst thou. Seem they grave and learnèd?
Why, so didst thou. Come they of noble family?
Why, so didst thou. Seem they religious?
Why, so didst thou. Or are they spare in diet,
Free from gross passion or of mirth or anger,
Constant in spirit, not swerving with the blood,
Garnished and decked in modest complement,
Not working with the eye without the ear,
And but in purgèd judgment trusting neither?
Such and so finely bolted didst thou seem.
And thus thy fall hath left a kind of blot
To mark the full-fraught man and best endued
With some suspicion. I will weep for thee,
For this revolt of thine methinks is like
Another fall of man.—Their faults are open.
Arrest them to the answer of the law,
And God acquit them of their practices.

from shreds and patches of righteousness. But the devil that tempted you gave you no reason why you should commit treason other than to win the name of traitor. The demon who seduced you could stride the world over with the proud gait of a lion, could return to hell and tell the devil's legions, "I will never win another soul as easily as I won that Englishman's." How you have poisoned my faith in people! Now I am suspicious of everyone. Are there men who appear dutiful? Why, so did you. Are there those who seem serious and knowledgeable? Why, so did you. Do they come from good families? Why, so did you. Do they seem religious? Why, so did you. Do they live in moderation, free from excessive emotion—stable rather than changing their minds constantly—tastefully dressed, not merely seeing but also listening, and trusting no impression without confirmation? That's how sound a man you appeared. Your fall has left a blot that opens even the best and brightest to suspicion. You have broken my heart. This treachery of yours is like the second Fall of man.—Their crimes are revealed. Arrest and punish them according to the law, and may God pardon them for what they would have done.

"Fall of man" refers to Adam and Eve's first sin—eating the fruit of the Tree of Knowledge, which caused them to lose their innocence and be expelled from Eden.

EXETER

I arrest thee of high treason, by the name of
Richard, Earl of Cambridge.
—I arrest thee of high treason, by the name of
Henry, Lord Scroop of Masham.
—I arrest thee of high treason, by the name of
Thomas Grey, knight, of Northumberland.

SCROOP

Our purposes God justly hath discovered,
And I repent my fault more than my death,
Which I beseech Your Highness to forgive,
Although my body pay the price of it.

CAMBRIDGE

For me, the gold of France did not seduce,
Although I did admit it as a motive
The sooner to effect what I intended;
But God be thankèd for prevention,
Which I in sufferance heartily will rejoice,
Beseeching God and you to pardon me.

GREY

Never did faithful subject more rejoice
At the discovery of most dangerous treason
Than I do at this hour joy o'er myself,
Prevented from a damnèd enterprise.
My fault, but not my body, pardon, sovereign.

KING HENRY

God quit you in His mercy. Hear your sentence:
You have conspired against our royal person,
Joined with an enemy proclaimed, and from his coffers
Received the golden earnest of our death,
Wherein you would have sold your king to slaughter,
His princes and his peers to servitude,
His subjects to oppression and contempt,
And his whole kingdom into desolation.
Touching our person, seek we no revenge,
But we our kingdom's safety must so tender,

EXETER

Richard Earl of Cambridge, I arrest you for high treason. Henry Lord Scroop of Masham, I arrest you for high treason. Thomas Grey, knight, of Northumberland, I arrest you for high treason.

SCROOP

A just God has discovered our plot. I regret my crime more than my death, and I beg your Highness to forgive me, while punishing my body with death.

CAMBRIDGE

For my part, I didn't do it for the money, though I admit the money encouraged me to do what I was planning sooner. But I thank God that I failed in my scheme, and I rejoice in paying the penalty, as I beg God and you to pardon me.

GREY

No faithful subject ever rejoiced more at the discovery of most dangerous treason than I now rejoice that I was thwarted in a damnable undertaking. Pardon my crime, sovereign, but not my person.

KING HENRY

May God in His mercy forgive you. This is your sentence. You have conspired against us with a proclaimed enemy and accepted his money in exchange for killing us. In doing so, you would have sold your king to slaughter, his princes and lords to slavery, his subjects to oppression and abuse, and his whole kingdom to ruin. I seek no revenge for myself, but so dearly do I hold the safety of my kingdom, which you sought to destroy, that you must be punished according to her laws. So go to your deaths, poor miserable

Whose ruin you have sought, that to her laws
We do deliver you. Get you therefore hence,
Poor miserable wretches, to your death,
The taste whereof God of His mercy give
You patience to endure, and true repentance
Of all your dear offences.—Bear them hence.

Exeunt CAMBRIDGE, SCROOP, *and* GREY, *guarded*

Now, lords, for France, the enterprise whereof
Shall be to you as us, like glorious.
We doubt not of a fair and lucky war,
Since God so graciously hath brought to light
This dangerous treason lurking in our way
To hinder our beginnings. We doubt not now
But every rub is smoothèd on our way.
Then forth, dear countrymen. Let us deliver
Our puissance into the hand of God,
Putting it straight in expedition.
Cheerly to sea. The signs of war advance.
No king of England if not king of France.

Exeunt

wretches, the pain of which may merciful God give you the strength to endure. And may you truly regret your terrible crimes. Take them away.

CAMBRIDGE, SCROOP, *and* GREY *exit under guard.*

And now, my lords, off to France. This invasion will be as glorious to you as it is to me. I have no doubt that it will be a swift and successful war, since God so graciously exposed this dangerous plot. I'm now sure that every bump in the road has been removed. Let's go forth, dear countrymen. Our strength is God. Let's get going. We're off to sea, banners flying. I'll be no king of England if I'm not also king of France.

They all exit.

ACT 2, SCENE 3

Enter PISTOL, HOSTESS, NYM, BARDOLPH, *and* BOY

HOSTESS

Prithee, honey-sweet husband, let me bring thee to Staines.

PISTOL

No; for my manly heart doth earn.—Bardolph, be blithe.—Nym, rouse thy vaunting veins.—Boy, bristle thy courage up. For Falstaff, he is dead, and we must earn therefore.

BARDOLPH

Would I were with him, wheresome'er he is, either in heaven or in hell.

HOSTESS

Nay, sure, he's not in hell! He's in Arthur's bosom, if ever man went to Arthur's bosom. He made a finer end, and went away an it had been any christom child. He parted ev'n just between twelve and one, ev'n at the turning o' th' tide; for after I saw him fumble with the sheets and play with flowers and smile upon his finger's end, I knew there was but one way, for his nose was as sharp as a pen, and he told of green fields. "How now, Sir John?" quoth I. "What, man, be o' good cheer!" So he cried out "God, God, God!" three or four times. Now I, to comfort him, bid him he should not think of God. I hoped there was no need to trouble himself with any such thoughts yet. So he bade me lay more clothes on his feet. I put my hand into the bed and felt them, and they were as cold as any stone. Then I felt to his knees, and so upward and upward, and all was as cold as any stone.

NYM

They say he cried out of sack.

HOSTESS

Ay, that he did.

ACT 2, SCENE 3

PISTOL, HOSTESS, NYM, BARDOLPH, *and* **BOY** *enter.*

HOSTESS

Please, sweet husband, let me come with you as far as the town of Staines.

PISTOL

No, because my manly heart is grieving. Bardolph, be happy.—Nym, rouse your bragging spirits.—Boy, be brave. Falstaff is dead, and we must mourn him.

BARDOLPH

I wish I were with him, wherever he is—in heaven or in hell.

HOSTESS

The hostess means Abraham's bosom, the proverbial resting place of good Christians, but has King Arthur on the brain.

Oh, no, he's surely not in hell. He's in Arthur's bosom, if any man ever went to Arthur's bosom. He died as peacefully as a baby. He departed right between twelve and one, just as the tide was turning. For after I saw him fumbling with the sheets and playing with imaginary flowers and smiling at the ends of his fingers, I knew it was the end. His face was gaunt and he was babbling about green fields. "Now, now, Sir John!" I said. "What's all this? Cheer up!" And he called out "God, God, God!" three or four times. To soothe him, I told him not to think of God, that I hoped it wasn't yet time to bother with such thoughts. So he asked me to put more blankets on his feet. I put my hand into the bed and felt his feet, and they were stone-cold. Then I felt his legs, and they were stone-cold, and so I moved upward and upward, and his whole body was stone-cold.

NYM

They say he cried out against sherry.

HOSTESS

Yes, he did.

BARDOLPH
And of women.

HOSTESS
Nay, that he did not.

BOY
Yes, that he did, and said they were devils incarnate.

HOSTESS
'A could never abide carnation. 'Twas a color he never liked.

BOY
He said once the devil would have him about women.

HOSTESS
He did in some sort, indeed, handle women, but then he was rheumatic, and talked of the Whore of Babylon.

BOY
Do you not remember he saw a flea stick upon Bardolph's nose, and he said it was a black soul burning in hell?

BARDOLPH
Well, the fuel is gone that maintained that fire. That's all the riches I got in his service.

NYM
Shall we shog? The King will be gone from Southampton.

PISTOL
Come, let's away.—My love, give me thy lips.
Look to my chattels and my movables.
Let senses rule. The word is "Pitch and pay."
Trust none, for oaths are straws, men's faiths are
wafer-cakes,
And Holdfast is the only dog, my duck.
Therefore, *caveto* be thy counselor.
Go, clear thy crystals.—Yoke-fellows in arms,

BARDOLPH

And women.

HOSTESS

No, he did not.

BOY

Yes, he did. He said they were devils incarnate.

HOSTESS

He could never bear carnation. It was a color he never did like.

BOY

He once said the devil would get him because of women.

HOSTESS

He did touch on women a bit, but his body was aching with fever and he talked about the Whore of Babylon.

BOY

Don't you remember how he saw a flea land on Bardolph's nose and said it was a black soul burning in hell?

BARDOLPH

The "fuel" Bardolph refers to is the drinks Falstaff bought him, which made his face even redder.

Well, the fuel that sustained that fire is gone. That's all the wealth I ever earned in his company.

NYM

Shall we get moving? The king will already have left Southampton.

PISTOL

Come, let's be on our way. My love, let me kiss your lips. Look after my goods and possessions. Keep on your toes: the rule is "cash down, no credit." Trust no one. For oaths are as easily broken as straws, and men's faith crumbles like crackers, and you can only rely on what you can hold onto. Let caution be your guide. Go dry your eyes. Brothers in arms, we're off to

Let us to France, like horse-leeches, my boys,
To suck, to suck, the very blood to suck.

BOY
And that's but unwholesome food, they say.

PISTOL
Touch her soft mouth, and march.

BARDOLPH
Farewell, hostess. *(kissing her)*

NYM
I cannot kiss, that is the humor of it. But adieu.

PISTOL
Let housewifery appear. Keep close, I thee command.

HOSTESS
Farewell. Adieu.

Exeunt

France—like leeches, my boys: to suck, to suck, their very blood to suck!

BOY

I've heard that's not the most nourishing food.

PISTOL

Kiss her soft mouth, and we'll be off.

BARDOLPH

Farewell, hostess. *(kisses her)*

NYM

I can't kiss—that's just how it is—but farewell.

PISTOL

Be thrifty. And keep yourself hidden, I command you.

HOSTESS

Farewell. Adieu.

They all exit.

ACT 2, SCENE 4

Flourish. Enter the KING OF FRANCE, *the* DAUPHIN, *the Dukes of Berri and Brittany, the* CONSTABLE, *and others*

KING OF FRANCE

Thus comes the English with full power upon us,
And more than carefully it us concerns
To answer royally in our defenses.
Therefore the Dukes of Berri and of Brittany,
Of Brabant and of Orléans, shall make forth,
And you, Prince Dauphin, with all swift dispatch,
To line and new-repair our towns of war
With men of courage and with means defendant.
For England his approaches makes as fierce
As waters to the sucking of a gulf.
It fits us then to be as provident
As fear may teach us out of late examples
Left by the fatal and neglected English
Upon our fields.

DAUPHIN

To view the sick and feeble parts of France.
And let us do it with no show of fear,
No, with no more than if we heard that England
Were busied with a Whitsun morris-dance.
For, my good liege, she is so idly kinged,
Her scepter so fantastically borne
By a vain, giddy, shallow, humorous youth,
That fear attends her not. My most redoubted father,
It is most meet we arm us 'gainst the foe,
For peace itself should not so dull a kingdom,
Though war nor no known quarrel were in question,
But that defenses, musters, preparations,
Should be maintained, assembled, and collected,
As were a war in expectation.
Therefore I say 'tis meet we all go forth

ACT 2, SCENE 4

Trumpets sound. The KING OF FRANCE, *the* DAUPHIN, *the* CONSTABLE, *the dukes of Berri and Bretagne, and others enter.*

KING OF FRANCE

The English army is advancing on us at full strength. It is more important that we respond majestically than that we respond carefully. Therefore the dukes of Berri, Bretagne, Brabant, and Orléans shall advance, and you, Prince Dauphin, will swiftly entrench and fortify our fortress towns with men of courage and the means to defend themselves. The king of England's approach is as forceful as a whirlpool. It is right for us to prepare like people who are afraid, as we've been taught by the recent lessons given us by the deadly and underestimated English on our own soil.

The king of France is referring to French defeats at Crécy (in 1346) and Poitiers (in 1356).

DAUPHIN

My most feared father, it is certainly appropriate for us to arm ourselves against the enemy, because even in peace time, when no war or conflict is at hand, a kingdom should not lose its edge, but always be ready—with defenses, men, and training—as though it expected a war. Therefore, I agree that we should all go and inspect those French territories that are weak. Let's do it with no show of anxiety—no, with no more fear than if we'd heard that the English were busying themselves with folk dancing. Because, my good king, England is so poorly led, her scepter so foolishly borne by a vain, silly, shallow, impulsive youth, that she's hardly a threat.

CONSTABLE

Oh peace, Prince Dauphin!
You are too much mistaken in this king.
Question your Grace the late ambassadors
With what great state he heard their embassy,
How well supplied with noble counselors,
How modest in exception, and withal
How terrible in constant resolution,
And you shall find his vanities forespent
Were but the outside of the Roman Brutus,
Covering discretion with a coat of folly,
As gardeners do with ordure hide those roots
That shall first spring and be most delicate.

DAUPHIN

Well, 'tis not so, my Lord High Constable.
But though we think it so, it is no matter.
In cases of defense 'tis best to weigh
The enemy more mighty than he seems.
So the proportions of defense are filled,
Which of a weak or niggardly projection
Doth, like a miser, spoil his coat with scanting
A little cloth.

KING OF FRANCE

Think we King Harry strong,
And, princes, look you strongly arm to meet him.
The kindred of him hath been fleshed upon us,
And he is bred out of that bloody strain
That haunted us in our familiar paths.
Witness our too-much-memorable shame
When Cressy battle fatally was struck
And all our princes captived by the hand
Of that black name, Edward, Black Prince of Wales,
Whiles that his mountain sire, on mountain standing

CONSTABLE

Oh, please, Prince Dauphin! You are completely wrong about this king. Talk to the ambassadors who've just come back: ask them how majestically he responded to their message, how well supplied he was with good advisors, how restrained in expressing his displeasure, and, moreover, how terrifyingly firm he was in his resolve. You'll discover that his youthful follies were like the persona that Lucius Junius Brutus adopted to deceive Tarquin—cloaking wisdom in folly the way gardeners cover the most delicate roots with manure when they first sprout up.

In Roman history, a nobleman named Lucius Junius Brutus pretended to be feebleminded so King Tarquin wouldn't recognize he was a threat.

DAUPHIN

Well, you're wrong, my Lord High Constable. But even if I thought you were right, it doesn't matter. When it comes to defense, it's best to assume that the enemy is more powerful than he seems. That way, we fill the gaps in our defenses. Otherwise, if we do it on the cheap, we'll be like the miser who spoils his new coat by not buying quite enough cloth to make it.

KING OF FRANCE

I think King Harry is strong, so the rest of you princes make sure to arm yourselves to meet him with strength. His ancestors got their first taste of blood in battle with us, and he is born of that warlike strain that haunted us on our home ground. Reflect on the battle of Crécy, where, to our everlasting shame, all our princes were taken prisoner by the Prince of Wales, he whom they called Edward the Black Prince. Remember how his mountain-bred father, standing high on a

Up in the air, crowned with the golden sun,
Saw his heroical seed and smiled to see him
Mangle the work of nature and deface
The patterns that by God and by French fathers
Had twenty years been made. This is a stem
Of that victorious stock, and let us fear
The native mightiness and fate of him.

Enter a MESSENGER

MESSENGER
Ambassadors from Harry King of England
Do crave admittance to your Majesty.

KING OF FRANCE
We'll give them present audience. Go, and bring them.

Exit MESSENGER

You see this chase is hotly followed, friends.

DAUPHIN
Turn head and stop pursuit, for coward dogs
Most spend their mouths when what they seem to threaten
Runs far before them. Good my sovereign,
Take up the English short, and let them know
Of what a monarchy you are the head.
Self-love, my liege, is not so vile a sin
As self-neglecting.

Enter EXETER *and train, and lords*

KING OF FRANCE
From our brother England?

EXETER
From him, and thus he greets your Majesty:
He wills you, in the name of God Almighty,
That you divest yourself and lay apart

mountain, crowned by the golden sun, observed his heroic son and smiled to see him mangle the work of nature, French youth whose fathers and God had nurtured for twenty years, since they were babies. This king is a branch of that same victorious stock. So let us be wary both of his inborn might and of his destiny.

A MESSENGER *enters.*

MESSENGER
Ambassadors of Harry, king of England, request a hearing with your Majesty.

KING OF FRANCE
We'll see them immediately. Bring them right in.

MESSENGER *and certain lords exit.*

Notice, my friends, how closely this hunter follows his prey.

DAUPHIN
Turn and face them and you'll stop the pursuit. The cowardly pack barks loudest when the quarry is way out front. My good King, surprise the English and let them know what kind of kingdom you rule over. Self-love, my liege, is not so great a sin as self-neglect.

The Lords and EXETER *enter with followers.*

KING OF FRANCE
From our brother monarch, the king of England?

EXETER
Yes, from him. Thus he greets your Majesty. He commands you, in the name of God: give up. Relinquish the stolen titles that, by the gift of heaven and the laws

The borrowed glories that, by gift of heaven,
By law of nature and of nations, 'longs
To him and to his heirs—namely, the crown
And all wide-stretchèd honors that pertain
By custom and the ordinance of times
Unto the crown of France. That you may know
'Tis no sinister nor no awkward claim
Picked from the wormholes of long-vanished days,
Nor from the dust of old oblivion raked,
He sends you this most memorable line,
In every branch truly demonstrative,
Willing you overlook this pedigree,
And when you find him evenly derived
From his most famed of famous ancestors,
Edward the Third, he bids you then resign
Your crown and kingdom, indirectly held
From him, the native and true challenger.

KING OF FRANCE
Or else what follows?

EXETER
Bloody constraint, for if you hide the crown
Even in your hearts, there will he rake for it.
Therefore in fierce tempest is he coming,
In thunder and in earthquake like a Jove,
That, if requiring fail, he will compel,
And bids you, in the bowels of the Lord,
Deliver up the crown and to take mercy
On the poor souls for whom this hungry war
Opens his vasty jaws, and on your head
Turning the widows' tears, the orphans' cries,
The dead men's blood, the pining maidens' groans,
For husbands, fathers, and betrothèd lovers,
That shall be swallowed in this controversy.
This is his claim, his threat'ning, and my message—
Unless the Dauphin be in presence here,
To whom expressly I bring greeting too.

of nature and of nations, belong to him and his heirs. That is, give up the crown and all the extensive titles that go with it, according to custom and long use. So that you'll know this is no dubious or farfetched claim, he sends you his family tree, every line of which supports the claim. Look over this document, and when you see that he is directly descended from his most famous of famous ancestors, Edward the Third, he demands that you resign your crown and kingdom, which you wrongfully hold at the expense of himself, the true and natural owner.

KING OF FRANCE

And what will happen if I don't?

EXETER

Bloodshed will force you to. No matter how deeply you hid the crown, even if you hid it in your own hearts, he'd dig it up. That's why he's coming after you like a fierce storm, with thunder and earthquakes like Jove could stir up. So, if asking you for the crown doesn't work, he will force you to give it to him. In the name of God, then, he asks that you deliver up the crown. He says to take pity on the poor souls whom this ravenous war will swallow up. The widows' tears, the orphans' cries, the dead men's blood, the girls mourning for their husbands, the fathers and the men they might have married will all be your fault. This is his claim, his threat, and my message. If the Dauphin is here, I have a message for him, too.

In Roman mythology, Jove (also known as Jupiter) was the king of the gods.

KING OF FRANCE
For us, we will consider of this further.
Tomorrow shall you bear our full intent
Back to our brother England.

DAUPHIN
For the Dauphin,
I stand here for him. What to him from England?

EXETER
Scorn and defiance, slight regard, contempt,
And anything that may not misbecome
The mighty sender, doth he prize you at.
Thus says my king: an if your father's Highness
Do not, in grant of all demands at large,
Sweeten the bitter mock you sent his Majesty,
He'll call you to so hot an answer of it
That caves and womby vaultages of France
Shall chide your trespass and return your mock
In second accent of his ordinance.

DAUPHIN
Say, if my father render fair return,
It is against my will, for I desire
Nothing but odds with England. To that end,
As matching to his youth and vanity,
I did present him with the Paris balls.

EXETER
He'll make your Paris Louvre shake for it,
Were it the mistress court of mighty Europe.
And be assured you'll find a difference,
As we his subjects have in wonder found,
Between the promise of his greener days
And these he masters now. Now he weighs time
Even to the utmost grain. That you shall read
In your own losses, if he stay in France.

KING OF FRANCE
Tomorrow shall you know our mind at full.

KING OF FRANCE

I'll think it over. Tomorrow, I'll let you know what I've decided and what answer you should deliver to the king of England.

DAUPHIN

Regarding the Dauphin, you can speak to me. What's the message from the English king?

EXETER

Scorn and defiance, indifference, contempt, and any insult that wouldn't disgrace the mighty sender—that's the value he puts on you. And my king goes on: if your royal father does not sweeten the bitter insult you sent my king and grant all our demands, Henry's artillery will give you so resounding an answer that the very caves and vaulted cathedrals of France shall echo your mocking of him back in your face.

DAUPHIN

Say this: if my father sends a friendly answer, it is against my will. I want nothing but conflict with England. To that end, I presented him with the tennis balls, the perfect expression of his inexperience and frivolity.

EXETER

He'll make your palace tremble for this insult, even if it were the mightiest in all of Europe. And, make no mistake, you'll find, as we his subjects have, an amazing difference between the king as a young man and the way he is now. Now he uses his time wisely, as you will see by your own casualties, if he remains in France.

KING OF FRANCE

We'll give you an answer tomorrow.

Flourish

EXETER
Dispatch us with all speed, lest that our king
Come here himself to question our delay,
For he is footed in this land already.

KING OF FRANCE
You shall be soon dispatched with fair conditions.
A night is but small breath and little pause
To answer matters of this consequence.

Flourish

Exeunt

A trumpet plays.

EXETER

Don't take too long, unless you want our king to come after me to ask what's holding things up, because he's already landed here.

KING OF FRANCE

You'll have your answer soon. A night isn't much time for addressing matters of this importance.

A trumpet sounds.

They all exit.

ACT THREE

PROLOGUE

Enter CHORUS

CHORUS

Thus with imagined wing our swift scene flies
In motion of no less celerity
Than that of thought. Suppose that you have seen
The well-appointed king at Hampton pier
Embark his royalty, and his brave fleet
With silken streamers the young Phoebus fanning.
Play with your fancies and in them behold,
Upon the hempen tackle, shipboys climbing.
Hear the shrill whistle, which doth order give
To sounds confused. Behold the threaden sails,
Borne with th' invisible and creeping wind,
Draw the huge bottoms through the furrowed sea,
Breasting the lofty surge. Oh, do but think
You stand upon the rivage and behold
A city on th' inconstant billows dancing,
For so appears this fleet majestical
Holding due course to Harfleur. Follow, follow!
Grapple your minds to sternage of this navy
And leave your England, as dead midnight still,
Guarded with grandsires, babies, and old women,
Either past or not arrived to pith and puissance,
For who is he whose chin is but enriched
With one appearing hair that will not follow
These culled and choice-drawn cavaliers to France?
Work, work your thoughts, and therein see a siege.
Behold the ordnance on their carriages,
With fatal mouths gaping on girded Harfleur.
Suppose th' Ambassador from the French comes back,
Tells Harry that the king doth offer him

ACT THREE

PROLOGUE

The CHORUS *enters.*

CHORUS

And so, on the wings of imagination and at the speed of thought, our scene flies swiftly on. Imagine that you have seen the well-equipped king at Dover pier set sail in full royal regalia and his noble fleet fan the rising sun with its silken banners. Give your imagination free rein. Picture the cabin boys climbing around the rigging. Hear the shrill whistle that brings order to the hubbub. Picture the linen sails driven by the invisible and subtle wind as they pull the vast hulls through the wrinkled sea, breasting the high waves. Pretend that you're standing on the shore, watching a city dance on the shifting waves, and you'll have an idea of the look of this majestic fleet as it holds a straight course for Harfleur. Follow it, follow it! Hitch your minds to this navy's sterns and leave your England, silent as midnight, guarded by grandfathers, babies, and old women. For what male subject is there old enough for his chin to be graced with even one hair who doesn't want to follow this select band of hand-picked knights to France? Once there, make your thoughts work harder, and witness a siege. Take in the wheeled canons with their deadly gaping mouths trained on the walled city of Harfleur. Imagine the French ambassador returning to inform Harry that the king offers him

Katherine his daughter and with her, to dowry,
Some petty and unprofitable dukedoms.
The offer likes not, and the nimble gunner
With linstock now the devilish cannon touches,

Alarum, and chambers go off

And down goes all before them. Still be kind
And eke out our performance with your mind.

Exit

his daughter, Katherine, with some insignificant, unprofitable dukedoms as her dowry. The offer doesn't go over well, and the nimble gunner now moves to ignite the devilish canon.

Sounds of battle and gunfire from offstage.

Down goes everything in their path. Indulge us further and supplement our performance with your own imaginings.

The CHORUS *exits.*

ACT 3, SCENE 1

Alarum

Enter KING HENRY, EXETER, BEDFORD, GLOUCESTER, *and soldiers, with scaling ladders*

KING HENRY

Once more unto the breach, dear friends, once more,
Or close the wall up with our English dead!
In peace there's nothing so becomes a man
As modest stillness and humility,
But when the blast of war blows in our ears,
Then imitate the action of the tiger:
Stiffen the sinews, summon up the blood,
Disguise fair nature with hard-favored rage,
Then lend the eye a terrible aspect,
Let pry through the portage of the head
Like the brass cannon, let the brow o'erwhelm it
As fearfully as doth a gallèd rock
O'erhang and jutty his confounded base,
Swilled with the wild and wasteful ocean.
Now set the teeth and stretch the nostril wide,
Hold hard the breath and bend up every spirit
To his full height. On, on, you noblest English,
Whose blood is fet from fathers of war-proof,
Fathers that, like so many Alexanders,
Have in these parts from morn till even fought
And sheathed their swords for lack of argument.
Dishonor not your mothers. Now attest
That those whom you called fathers did beget you.
Be copy now to men of grosser blood,
And teach them how to war. And you, good yeoman,
Whose limbs were made in England, show us here
The mettle of your pasture. Let us swear
That you are worth your breeding, which I doubt not,

ACT 3, SCENE 1

Sounds of battle.

KING HENRY *enters, with* EXETER, BEDFORD, GLOUCESTER, *and soldiers carrying ladders for scaling the walls that surround Harfleur.*

KING HENRY

Attack the breach in the city wall once more, dear friends, attack it once more—or else let's close it up with English corpses. In peacetime, nothing looks better in a man than restraint and humility. But when the battle trumpet blows in our ears, then it's time to act like the tiger. With muscles taut and blood stirred up, hide your civilized nature under the guise of ugly rage. Lend your eyes a terrifying gleam and let them jut out from the portholes of the head like brass cannon. Make your brow jut out over your eyes like a frightening cliff over the wild and desolate ocean. Now grit your teeth and let your nostrils flare. Take a deep breath and draw on every impulse to its fullest strength. On, on, you noblest Englishmen, descended as you are from battle-tested fathers, fathers who, like so many Alexander the Greats, have fought in these regions from morning until night, sheathing their swords only when there was no one left to fight. Don't dishonor your mothers! Prove that the men you call your fathers did truly conceive you. Serve as an example to men of common birth and teach them how to fight. And you, good farmers, whose limbs were made in England, show us here the vigor of your upbringing. Prove you are worthy of your birth, which I do not doubt for a moment. For there isn't one of you so lowborn that your eyes don't shine with noble luster. I see

For there is none of you so mean and base
That hath not noble luster in your eyes.
I see you stand like greyhounds in the slips,
Straining upon the start. The game's afoot.
Follow your spirit, and upon this charge
Cry "God for Harry, England, and Saint George!"

Alarum, and chambers go off

Exeunt

you're standing like greyhounds on a leash, straining for the moment when you'll be let loose. The hunt is on! Follow your spirit, and as you charge cry, "God for Harry, England, and Saint George!"

They all exit to the sounds of battle and gunfire from offstage.

ACT 3, SCENE 2

Enter **NYM**, **BARDOLPH**, **PISTOL**, *and* **BOY**

BARDOLPH
On, on, on, on, on! To the breach, to the breach!

NYM
Pray thee, corporal, stay. The knocks are too hot, and, for mine own part, I have not a case of lives. The humor of it is too hot; that is the very plainsong of it.

PISTOL
"The plainsong" is most just, for humors do abound.
(sings)
Knocks go and come. God's vassals drop and die,
And sword and shield
In bloody field
Doth win immortal fame.

BOY
Would I were in an alehouse in London! I would give all my fame for a pot of ale, and safety.

PISTOL
And I.
(sings)
If wishes would prevail with me,
My purpose should not fail with me,
But thither would I hie.

BOY
(sings)
As duly,
But not as truly,
As bird doth sing on bough.

Enter **FLUELLEN**

FLUELLEN
Up to the breach, you dogs! Avaunt, you cullions!

ACT 3, SCENE 2

NYM, BARDOLPH, PISTOL, *and the* BOY *enter.*

BARDOLPH

On, on, on, on, on! To the breach, to the breach!

NYM

Please, corporal, stop! The fighting is too violent. Speaking for myself, I only have one life, not dozens. Too violent! That's just how it is, the plain truth of it.

PISTOL

The plain truth doesn't lie. You can see how it is all around. Fighting comes and goes, God's loyal servants drop and die. *(he sings)*

And sword and shield
In bloody field
Will win immortal fame.

BOY

I wish I were in an alehouse in London! I would give all my glory for a mug of ale and safety.

PISTOL

Me too. *(he sings)*

If wishes could avail me,
My purpose would not fail me,
It's there that I would go.

BOY

(singing)

As surely but more poorly
Than birds sing on the bough.

FLUELLEN *enters.*

FLUELLEN

Up to the breach, you dogs! Go! Get a move on, you scrotems!

PISTOL

Be merciful, great duke, to men of mold. Abate thy rage, abate thy manly rage, abate thy rage, great duke. Good bawcock, 'bate thy rage. Use lenity, sweet chuck.

NYM

These be good humors. Your Honor wins bad humors.

Exeunt all but BOY

BOY

As young as I am, I have observed these three swashers. I am boy to them all three, but all they three, though they would serve me, could not be man to me. For indeed three such antics do not amount to a man: for Bardolph, he is white-livered and red-faced, by the means whereof he faces it out but fights not; for Pistol, he hath a killing tongue and a quiet sword, by the means whereof he breaks words and keeps whole weapons; for Nym, he hath heard that men of few words are the best men, and therefore he scorns to say his prayers, lest he should be thought a coward, but his few bad words are matched with as few good deeds, for he never broke any man's head but his own, and that was against a post when he was drunk. They will steal anything and call it purchase. Bardolph stole a lute case, bore it twelve leagues, and sold it for three halfpence. Nym and Bardolph are sworn brothers in filching, and in Calais they stole a fire shovel. I knew by that piece of service the men would carry coals. They would have me as familiar with men's pockets as their gloves or their handkerchers, which makes much against my manhood, if I should take from another's pocket to put into mine, for it is plain pocketing up of wrongs. I must leave them and seek some better service. Their villainy goes against my weak stomach, and therefore I must cast it up.

Exit

PISTOL

Great Duke, be merciful to mortal men. Calm your rage, your manly rage! Calm your rage, great Duke! Dear man, calm your rage. Be lenient, dearest!

NYM

This is healthy talk. Your Honor's is unhealthy talk.

Everyone but the BOY *exits.*

BOY

Young though I am, I've been observing these three blowhards closely. I am "man"—which is to say, servant—to all three of them. Yet not one among them, if all three were to wait on me, could be my "man," because three such fakes don't amount to a man. Take Bardolph: he is cowardly and blustery. He acts tough, but he doesn't fight. Pistol, meanwhile, has a lethal tongue but an inert sword. He destroys words but keeps his weapon in one piece. As for Nym, he's heard men of valor are men of few words, so he refuses to pray lest he should be thought a coward. But he has as few good deeds as he has bad words—for he never cracked anyone's head but his own, and that was against a post when he was drunk. They will steal anything and call it spoils. Bardolph stole a lute case, carried it for thirty-six miles, and sold it for a penny and a half. Nym and Bardolph are sworn brothers in crime, and in Calais they stole a fire shovel: I could see from that that they had no pride. They would like me to be as familiar with men's pockets as their gloves and handkerchiefs, which goes against my manhood, because to take something from another's pocket and put it into my own is plain stealing. I must leave them and seek some better employment. Their villainy nauseates me, and I must therefore vomit it up.

He exits.

Enter FLUELLEN *and* GOWER

GOWER
Captain Fluellen, you must come presently to the mines; the duke of Gloucester would speak with you.

FLUELLEN
To the mines? Tell you the duke it is not so good to come to the mines, for, look you, the mines is not according to the disciplines of the war. The concavities of it is not sufficient, for, look you, th' athversary, you may discuss unto the duke, look you, is digt himself four yard under the countermines. By Cheshu, I think he will plow up all if there is not better directions.

GOWER
The duke of Gloucester, to whom the order of the siege is given, is altogether directed by an Irishman, a very valiant gentleman, i' faith.

FLUELLEN
It is Captain Macmorris, is it not?

GOWER
I think it be.

FLUELLEN
By Cheshu, he is an ass, as in the world. I will verify as much in his beard. He has no more directions in the true disciplines of the wars, look you, of the Roman disciplines, than is a puppy dog.

Enter Captain MACMORRIS *and Captain* JAMY

GOWER
Here he comes, and the Scots captain, Captain Jamy, with him.

FLUELLEN *enters, with* **GOWER** *following.*

GOWER

Captain Fluellen, you must come straight to the tunnels. The duke of Gloucester wants a word with you.

FLUELLEN

The tunnels! Tell the duke I'm not so keen to come to the tunnels. For the tunnels, see, are not strictly in accordance with the proper practice of war. They're not deep enough. For the enemy, see—and you can explain this to the duke, see—has dug its own tunnels four yards below ours. By Jesus, I think they will blow up everything if we don't improve our tactics.

GOWER

The duke of Gloucester, who has command over the siege, is in consultation with an Irishman, a very valiant gentleman indeed.

FLUELLEN

It's Captain Macmorris, right?

GOWER

I think so.

FLUELLEN

Jesus, he's an ass if there ever was one! I will say as much to his face. He knows no more about the proper practice of war, see—the ancient practices—than a puppy.

Captain **MACMORRIS** *and Captain* **JAMY** *enter.*

GOWER

Here he comes with Captain Jamy, the Scots captain.

FLUELLEN

Captain Jamy is a marvelous falorous gentleman, that is certain, and of great expedition and knowledge in th' aunchient wars, upon my particular knowledge of his directions. By Cheshu, he will maintain his argument as well as any military man in the world in the disciplines of the pristine wars of the Romans.

JAMY

I say gudday, Captain Fluellen.

FLUELLEN

Godden to your Worship, good Captain James.

GOWER

How now, Captain Macmorris, have you quit the mines? Have the pioneers given o'er?

MACMORRIS

By Chrish, la, 'tish ill done. The work ish give over. The trompet sound the retreat. By my hand I swear, and my father's soul, the work ish ill done. It ish give over. I would have blowed up the town, so Chrish save me, la, in an hour. Oh, 'tish ill done, 'tish ill done, by my hand, 'tish ill done.

FLUELLEN

Captain Macmorris, I beseech you now, will you voutsafe me, look you, a few disputations with you as partly touching or concerning the disciplines of the war, the Roman wars? In the way of argument, look you, and friendly communication, partly to satisfy my opinion, and partly for the satisfaction, look you, of my mind, as touching the direction of the military discipline, that is the point.

JAMY

It sall be vary gud, gud feith, gud captens bath, and I sall quit you with gud leve, as I may pick occasion, that sall I, marry.

FLUELLEN

Captain Jamy is a wonderfully valorous gentleman, that's certain, one with great learning and knowledge concerning ancient warfare, I happen to know from his maneuvers. By Jesus, he will defend his position on the practices of the ancient Roman wars as well as any military man in the world.

JAMY

Good day to you, Captain Fluellen.

FLUELLEN

Good evening to your Worship, good Captain James.

GOWER

Tell me, Captain Macmorris, have you left the tunnels? Have the excavators stopped work?

MACMORRIS

Christ, it's a disaster. The work is stopped, the trumpet has sounded the retreat. I swear by this hand and my father's soul, the whole thing is a disaster. It's all stopped. I could have blown up the town in an hour. Oh, it's a disaster, a disaster, by this hand, it's a disaster.

FLUELLEN

Captain Macmorris, I beg your pardon, but would you grant me a discussion or two with you, see, partly touching on or concerning the practice of war, the Roman wars, for the sake of argument, see, and friendly conversation? Partly to confirm my opinion and partly for the satisfaction, see, of my mind, with respect to the demands of proper military practice—that's the point?

JAMY

Oh, this is fine, good captains. And I'll answer you, if I may, when I get a chance. Indeed I will.

MACMORRIS

It is no time to discourse, so Chrish save me. The day is hot, and the weather, and the wars, and the king, and the dukes. It is no time to discourse. The town is beseeched, and the trumpet call us to the breach, and we talk and, be Chrish, do nothing, 'tis shame for us all. So God sa' me, 'tis shame to stand still. It is shame, by my hand. And there is throats to be cut and works to be done, and there ish nothing done, so Chrish sa' me, la.

JAMY

By the mess, ere theise eyes of mine take themselves to slomber, ay'll de gud service, or I'll lig i' th' grund for it, ay, or go to death. And I'll pay 't as valorously as I may, that sall I suerly do, that is the breff and the long. Marry, I wad full fain heard some question 'tween you tway.

FLUELLEN

Captain Macmorris, I think, look you, under your correction, there is not many of your nation—

MACMORRIS

Of my nation? What ish my nation? Ish a villain and a basterd and a knave and a rascal. What ish my nation? Who talks of my nation?

FLUELLEN

Look you, if you take the matter otherwise than is meant, Captain Macmorris, peradventure I shall think you do not use me with that affability as, in discretion, you ought to use me, look you, being as good a man as yourself, both in the disciplines of war and in the derivation of my birth and in other particularities.

MACMORRIS

I do not know you so good a man as myself. So Chrish save me, I will cut off your head.

GOWER

Gentlemen both, you will mistake each other.

MACMORRIS

This is no time to have a discussion. Christ! The day is hot and between the weather and the wars and the king and the dukes, it's no time for a discussion. The town is besieged, and the trumpet calls us to the gap, and we talk and do nothing, by Christ. It's a disgrace to us all. God save me, it's a disgrace, by this hand, when there are throats to be cut and work to be done, and nothing gets done, Christ save me.

JAMY

I swear by the mass, before I close my eyes to go to sleep, I'll put in some good fighting, or I'll lie in the ground dead. And I'll kill as valiantly as I can, that's for sure. That is the long and the short of it. But truly, I would love to hear the two of you discuss warfare.

FLUELLEN

Captain Macmorris, I think, see—correct me if I'm wrong—there are not many of your nation—

MACMORRIS

My nation? What is my nation? It's a villain and a bastard and a coward and a rascal. What is my nation? Who talks of my nation?

FLUELLEN

Captain Macmorris, if you take my words in some way other than how they were meant, see, I'll have to think you're not treating me with the good will you ought to, see, since I am as good a man as yourself, both in the practice of war and in my country of origin and in other respects.

MACMORRIS

I do not know that you are as good a man as myself. So, by Christ, I'll cut off your head.

GOWER

Now, now, both of you gentlemen! You go out of your way to misunderstand each other.

JAMY

Ah, that's a foul fault.

A parley sounds

GOWER

The town sounds a parley.

FLUELLEN

Captain Macmorris, when there is more better opportunity to be required, look you, I will be so bold as to tell you I know the disciplines of war, and there is an end.

Exeunt

JAMY

Yes, and that's a serious failing.

A trumpet tune that indicates a request for a ceasefire sounds.

GOWER

The town is asking for a pause in the fighting for negotiation.

FLUELLEN

Captain Macmorris, when we have more leisure, see, I will be so bold as to show you I know about the practice of warfare, and that's that.

They all exit.

ACT 3, SCENE 3

Enter the GOVERNOR *and some citizens on the walls. Enter* KING HENRY *and his train before the gates*

KING HENRY

How yet resolves the governor of the town?
This is the latest parle we will admit.
Therefore to our best mercy give yourselves
Or, like to men proud of destruction,
Defy us to our worst. For, as I am a soldier,
A name that in my thoughts becomes me best,
If I begin the batt'ry once again,
I will not leave the half-achieved Harfleur
Till in her ashes she lie burièd.
The gates of mercy shall be all shut up,
And the fleshed soldier, rough and hard of heart,
In liberty of bloody hand, shall range
With conscience wide as hell, mowing like grass
Your fresh fair virgins and your flow'ring infants.
What is it then to me if impious war,
Arrayed in flames like to the prince of fiends,
Do with his smirched complexion all fell feats
Enlinked to waste and desolation?
What is 't to me, when you yourselves are cause,
If your pure maidens fall into the hand
Of hot and forcing violation?
What rein can hold licentious wickedness
When down the hill he holds his fierce career?
We may as bootless spend our vain command
Upon th' enragèd soldiers in their spoil
As send precepts to the Leviathan
To come ashore. Therefore, you men of Harfleur,
Take pity of your town and of your people
Whiles yet my soldiers are in my command,
Whiles yet the cool and temperate wind of grace

ACT 3, SCENE 3

The GOVERNOR *and some citizens appear on the walls, the English army below.* KING HENRY *and his train enter.*

KING HENRY

What has the governor of the town decided? This is the final discussion I will grant. So submit to my mercy or, like men who revel in their own destruction, challenge me to do my worst. For, as I am a soldier, the name I think suits me best, once I begin my attack on Harfleur again, I will not leave the half-conquered town until she lies buried in her own ashes. The gates of mercy will be closed by then, and harsh and hard-hearted soldiers, who have tasted blood, will have free reign to commit whatever violence they want, mowing down your lovely young virgins and budding infants. What will it matter to me, since you will have brought it on yourselves, if sacrilegious war, dressed in red like Satan, his face blackened by smoke, should commit every form of savage destruction and ruin? What will it matter to me if your innocent maidens are raped, since you will have asked for it? What power can rein in promiscuous evil once it's gotten rolling? We might as well send orders to the whale to come ashore as try to restore order in soldiers carried away with their looting. Therefore, you men of Harfleur, take pity on your town and on your people while I still have control over my men, while the cool and moderate winds of mercy still have power to disperse the depraved, infected clouds of murder, plunder, and crazed soldiers defile your shrieking daughters with their foul hands, and your fathers dragged by their silver beards, their reverend heads dashed against the walls. Expect to see your naked babies skewered upon

O'erblows the filthy and contagious clouds
Of heady murder, spoil, and villainy.
If not, why, in a moment look to see
The blind and bloody soldier with foul hand
Desire the locks of your shrill-shrieking daughters,
Your fathers taken by the silver beards
And their most reverend heads dashed to the walls,
Your naked infants spitted upon pikes
Whiles the mad mothers with their howls confused
Do break the clouds, as did the wives of Jewry
At Herod's bloody-hunting slaughtermen.
What say you? Will you yield and this avoid
Or, guilty in defense, be thus destroyed?

GOVERNOR
Our expectation hath this day an end.
The Dauphin, whom of succors we entreated,
Returns us that his powers are yet not ready
To raise so great a siege. Therefore, great King,
We yield our town and lives to thy soft mercy.
Enter our gates, dispose of us and ours,
For we no longer are defensible.

KING HENRY
Open your gates.

Exit **GOVERNOR**

Come, uncle Exeter,
Go you and enter Harfleur. There remain
And fortify it strongly 'gainst the French.
Use mercy to them all for us, dear uncle,
The winter coming on and sickness growing
Upon our soldiers, we will retire to Calais.
Tonight in Harfleur will we be your guest;
Tomorrow for the march are we addressed.

Flourish, and enter the town

pikes while their grief-crazed mothers tear the clouds with their loud cries, just as the women of Judea did when Herod slaughtered their infants. What do you say? Will you surrender and avoid all this or be called to account for the destruction of this town?

GOVERNOR

Today our hopes are at an end. The Dauphin, whom we asked for reinforcements, sends back the answer that he's not yet in a position to raise so great an army. Therefore, great king, we surrender our town and lives to your kind mercy. Enter our gates and do as you like with us and our possessions, for we cannot defend ourselves any longer.

KING HENRY

Open your gates.

The GOVERNOR *exits.*

Come, uncle Exeter, enter Harfleur. Stay there and fortify it well against the French. Deal with them all mercifully on my behalf, dear uncle. Meanwhile, with winter coming on and sickness growing among our troops, we'll withdraw to Calais. Tonight in Harfleur we will be your guest; tomorrow we'll march on.

Trumpets. The KING *and his train enter the town.*

ACT 3, SCENE 4

Enter KATHERINE *and* ALICE

KATHERINE
Alice, tu as été en Angleterre, et tu parles bien le langage.

ALICE
Un peu, madame.

KATHERINE
Je te prie, m'enseignez. Il faut que j'apprenne à parler. Comment appelez-vous la main *en anglais?*

ALICE
La main? *Elle est appelée "de hand."*

KATHERINE
"De hand." Et les doigts?

ALICE
Les doigts? *Ma foi, j'oublie les doigts; mais je me souviendrai.* Les doigts? *Je pense qu'ils sont appelés* "de fingres"*; oui,* "de fingres."

KATHERINE
La main, "de hand"; *les doigts,* "de fingres." *Je pense que je suis le bon écolier. J'ai gagné deux mots d'anglais vitement. Comment appelez-vous* les ongles?

ALICE
Les ongles? *Nous les appelons "de nails."*

KATHERINE
"De nails." *Écoutez. Dites-moi si je parle bien*: "de hand, de fingres, et de nails."

ALICE
C'est bien dit, madame. Il est fort bon anglais.

KATHERINE
Dites-moi l'anglais pour le bras.

ALICE
"De arme," madame.

ACT 3, SCENE 4

KATHERINE *and* ALICE *enter.*

KATHERINE

(speaking in French, for the entire scene) Alice, you have been to England and you know the language.

ALICE

(speaking in French, for the entire scene) A little, madam.

KATHERINE

Please teach me English. I must learn to speak it. What is the word for *la main* in English?

ALICE

La main? That is "de hand."

KATHERINE

"De hand." And *les doigts*?

ALICE

Les doigts? Good lord, I forget *les doigts.* But it will come to me. The word for *les doigts,* I believe, is "de fangres." Yes, "de fangres."

KATHERINE

La main, "de hand"; *les doigts,* "de fangres." I think I am a very apt student! I have learned two words of English already. What is the word for *les ongles*?

ALICE

"*Les ongles?*" That is "de nails."

KATHERINE

"De nails." Listen! Tell me if I'm saying it right. De hand, de fangres, et de nails."

ALICE

Well done, madam. Excellent English.

KATHERINE

Tell me the English for *le bras.*

ALICE

"De arm," madam.

KATHERINE
Et le coude?

ALICE
"D'elbow."

KATHERINE
"D'elbow." *Je m'en fais la répétition de tous les mots que vous m'avez appris dès à présent.*

ALICE
Il est trop difficile, madame, comme je pense.

KATHERINE
Excusez-moi, Alice. Écoutez: "de hand, de fingres, de nails, de arma, de bilbow."

ALICE
"D'elbow," *madame.*

KATHERINE
Ô Seigneur Dieu! Je m'en oublie; "d'elbow." Comment *appelez-vous* le col?

ALICE
"De nick," *madame.*

KATHERINE
"De nick." *Et le menton?*

ALICE
"De chin."

KATHERINE
"De sin." *Le col,* "de nick"; *le menton,* "de sin."

ALICE
Oui. Sauf votre honneur, en vérité, vous prononcez les mots aussi droit que les natifs d'Angleterre.

KATHERINE
Je ne doute point d'apprendre, par la grâce de Dieu, et en peu de temps.

ALICE
N'avez vous pas déjà oublié ce que je vous ai enseigné?

KATHERINE
Non, je réciterai à vous promptement: "de hand, de fingre, de nails—"

KATHERINE

And *le coud*?

ALICE

"D'elbow."

KATHERINE

"D'elbow." Let me practice all the words you've taught me so far.

ALICE

It's too difficult, I think, madam.

KATHERINE

I beg to differ, Alice. Listen: "de hand, de fangres, de nails, d'arma, de bilbow."

ALICE

"D'elbow," madam.

KATHERINE

Oh, Lord, I forgot! "D'elbow." What is the word for *le col*?

ALICE

"De neck," madam.

KATHERINE

"De nick." And *le menton*?

ALICE

"De chin."

KATHERINE

Le col, "de nick"; *le menton,* "de sin."

ALICE

Yes. If I may say so, your Highness pronounces the words just like a native English speaker.

KATHERINE

I have no doubt I'll learn it, and in a short time, too—God willing.

ALICE

You haven't forgotten what you just learned?

KATHERINE

No, I'll recite it for you right now: "de hand, de fangres, de nails—"

ALICE
"De nails," *madame.*

KATHERINE
"De nails, de arme, de ilbow."

ALICE
Sauf votre honneur, "d'elbow."

KATHERINE
Ainsi dis-je: "d'elbow, de nick, et de sin." *Comment appelez-vous le pied et la robe?*

ALICE
"Le foot," *madame, et* "le count."

KATHERINE
"Le foot" *et* "de count." *Ô Seigneur Dieu! Ils sont mots de son mauvais, corruptible, gros, et impudique, et non pour les dames d'honneur d'user. Je ne voudrais prononcer ces mots devant les seigneurs de France pour tout le monde. Foh!* "Le foot" *et* "le count"! *Néanmoins, je réciterai une autre fois ma leçon ensemble*: "d' hand, de fingre, de nails, d' arme, d'elbow, de nick, de sin, de foot, le count."

ALICE
Excellent, madame!

KATHERINE
C'est assez pour une fois: Allons-nous à dîner.

Exeunt

ALICE

"De nails," madame.

KATHERINE

"De nails, de arme, de ilbow."

ALICE

Forgive me, de *el*bow.

KATHERINE

That's what I said, "de elbow, de nick, et de sin." What are the words for *le pied* and *la robe*?

ALICE

By "count," Alice means "gown."

"De foot," madame, and "de count."

KATHERINE

"Foot" and "count" sound to Katherine like the French foutre and con: to have sex and vagina, respectively.

"De foot" and "de count"! Oh, Lord, those are vulgar words—wicked, ugly, immodest, not fitting for respectable girls to speak. I would not utter those words in the presence of the lords of France for all the world. Ugh! "Le foot" and "le count"! Nevertheless, I will recite my lesson one more time all together: "de hand, de fangres, de nails, de arm, de elbow, de nick, de sin, de foot, de coun."

ALICE

That is excellent, madame!

KATHERINE

That's enough for one lesson. Let's go to lunch.

They exit.

ACT 3, SCENE 5

Enter the KING OF FRANCE, *the* DAUPHIN, *the duke of* BOURBON, *the* CONSTABLE *of France, and others*

KING OF FRANCE
'Tis certain he hath passed the river Somme.

CONSTABLE
An if he be not fought withal, my lord,
Let us not live in France. Let us quit all
And give our vineyards to a barbarous people.

DAUPHIN
Ô Dieu vivant, shall a few sprays of us,
The emptying of our fathers' luxury,
Our scions, put in wild and savage stock,
Spurt up so suddenly into the clouds
And overlook their grafters?

BOURBON
Normans, but bastard Normans, Norman bastards!
Mort de ma vie, if they march along
Unfought withal, but I will sell my dukedom
To buy a slobb'ry and a dirty farm
In that nook-shotten isle of Albion.

CONSTABLE
Dieu de batailles, where have they this mettle?
Is not their climate foggy, raw, and dull,
On whom, as in despite, the sun looks pale,
Killing their fruit with frowns? Can sodden water,
A drench for sur-reined jades, their barley broth,

ACT 3, SCENE 5

The KING OF FRANCE, *the* DAUPHIN, *the duke of* BOURBON, *and the* CONSTABLE *of France enter, with others.*

KING OF FRANCE

He's certainly crossed the river Somme.

CONSTABLE

And if he advances unopposed, my lord, let us abandon France. Let us leave everything and give our vineyards to the barbarous nation.

DAUPHIN

God alive! Shall a few offshoots of our nation, born of our father's lust—our branches grafted to wild and savage trunks—grow to such a height that they look down with contempt on the plants from which they first sprang?

The Dauphin is referring to the Norman invasion of 1066, in which William the Conqueror and natives of Normandy conquered England.

BOURBON

Normans, nothing more than bastard Normans, Norman bastards! I hope I die! If they march along unopposed, I will sell my dukedom for a sodden, filthy farm in that craggy isle of Albion.

CONSTABLE

God of battles! Where do they get this spirit? Isn't their climate foggy, cold, and dark? Doesn't the sun shine palely down on them, as though in contempt, killing their fruit with frowns? Can boiled water (beer, they call it)—a drink for broken-down horses, heat their cold blood to such a valiant level? And shall our

Decoct their cold blood to such valiant heat?
And shall our quick blood, spirited with wine,
Seem frosty? Oh, for honor of our land,
Let us not hang like roping icicles
Upon our houses' thatch, whiles a more frosty people
Sweat drops of gallant youth in our rich fields!
"Poor" we may call them in their native lords.

DAUPHIN

By faith and honor,
Our madams mock at us and plainly say
Our mettle is bred out and they will give
Their bodies to the lust of English youth
To new-store France with bastard warriors.

BOURBON

And teach lavoltas high, and swift corantos,
Saying our grace is only in our heels
And that we are most lofty runaways. They bid us to the
English dancing schools.

KING OF FRANCE

Where is Montjoy the herald? Speed him hence.
Let him greet England with our sharp defiance.
Up, princes, and, with spirit of honor edged
More sharper than your swords, hie to the field:
Charles Delabreth, High Constable of France;
You dukes of Orléans, Bourbon, and of Berri,
Alençon, Brabant, Bar, and Burgundy;
Jacques Chatillon, Rambures, Vaudemont,
Beaumont, Grandpré, Roussi, and Faulconbridge,
Foix, Lestrale, Bouciqualt, and Charolois;
High dukes, great princes, barons, lords, and knights,
For your great seats now quit you of great shames.
Bar Harry England, that sweeps through our land
With pennons painted in the blood of Harfleur.
Rush on his host, as doth the melted snow
Upon the valleys, whose low vassal seat

lively blood, quickened by wine, be so frosty? Oh, for the honor of our land, let us not hang like ropes of icicles off the thatched roofs of our houses while men of a more frosty temperament sweat off their own gallant youth in our rich fields! Our fields may be rich, but they are ruled poorly.

DAUPHIN

By faith and honor, our wives mock us, telling us brazenly that our vigor has been so bred out of us that they plan to give their bodies to the lusty youth of England to resupply France with men who, though bastards, will at least be warriors.

BOURBON

They tell us we'd be better off in English dancing schools, where we could teach the latest dances, as our grace is all in our heels; we are no better than high-class deserters.

KING OF FRANCE

Where is Montjoy, the herald? Send him on his way quickly. Tell him to greet the king of England with our sharp defiance. Rise, princes, and, with a spirit of honor more sharply edged than your swords, rush to the battlefield: Charles Delabreth, High Constable of France; you dukes of Orléans, Bourbon, Berri, Alençon, Brabant, Bar, and Burgundy; Jaques Chatillon, Rambures, Vaudemont, Beaumont, Grandpré, Roussi, and Fauconberg, Foix, Lestrale, Bouciqualt, and Charolois. High dukes, great princes, barons, lords and knights—for the sake of the great positions you hold, rid yourselves of this great shame. Stop Harry of England, who is now sweeping through our land with banners drenched in the French blood he spilled at Harfleur. Rush on his army the way the melting snow of the Alps spits on the low valleys

The Alps doth spit and void his rheum upon.
Go down upon him—you have power enough—
And in a captive chariot into Rouen
Bring him our prisoner.

CONSTABLE
This becomes the great!
Sorry am I his numbers are so few,
His soldiers sick and famished in their march,
For, I am sure, when he shall see our army
He'll drop his heart into the sink of fear
And for achievement offer us his ransom.

KING OF FRANCE
Therefore, Lord Constable, haste on Montjoy
And let him say to England that we send
To know what willing ransom he will give.
—Prince Dauphin, you shall stay with us in Rouen.

DAUPHIN
Not so, I do beseech your Majesty.

KING OF FRANCE
Be patient, for you shall remain with us.
—Now forth, Lord Constable and princes all,
And quickly bring us word of England's fall.

Exeunt

below them. Descend on him: you have power enough. And bring him into Rouen as our prisoner.

CONSTABLE

Now that's a mission worthy of great men! I'm only sorry that his numbers are so few and those men he has sick and starving on the march. When he sees our army, I'm sure his heart will sink with fear and he'll offer us a large sum in exchange for avoiding battleof.

KING OF FRANCE

Have Montjoy hurry, then, Lord Constable, and have him ask the king of England what he is willing to pay us to get out of the war. Prince Dauphin, you'll stay with me in Rouen.

DAUPHIN

No, please, I beg your Majesty.

KING OF FRANCE

Be patient, because you're staying with me. Go now, Lord Constable and all you princes, and quickly bring us news of England's defeat.

They all exit.

ACT 3, SCENE 6

Enter GOWER *and* FLUELLEN, *meeting*

GOWER
How now, Captain Fluellen? Come you from the bridge?

FLUELLEN
I assure you, there is very excellent services committed at the bridge.

GOWER
Is the duke of Exeter safe?

FLUELLEN
The duke of Exeter is as magnanimous as Agamemnon, and a man that I love and honor with my soul and my heart and my duty and my life and my living and my uttermost power. He is not, God be praised and blessed, any hurt in the world, but keeps the bridge most valiantly, with excellent discipline. There is an aunchient lieutenant there at the pridge. I think in my very conscience he is as valiant a man as Mark Antony, and he is a man of no estimation in the world, but I did see him do as gallant service.

GOWER
What do you call him?

FLUELLEN
He is called Aunchient Pistol.

GOWER
I know him not.

Enter PISTOL

FLUELLEN
Here is the man.

ACT 3, SCENE 6

GOWER and FLUELLEN enter from opposite sides of the stage.

GOWER

Greetings, Captain Fluellen! Have you just come from the bridge?

FLUELLEN

I assure you, there are some excellent military operations being carried out at the bridge.

GOWER

Is the duke of Exeter safe?

FLUELLEN

Agamemnon was the leader of the Greek army in the Trojan War. Mark Antony fought Brutus for control of theRoman Empire.

The duke of Exeter is as courageous as Agamemnon and a man whom I love and honor deeply, with my soul, and my heart, and my duty, and my life, and my livelihood, to the very utmost of my being. He is not—God be praised and blessed—hurt in any way but is holding the bridge most valiantly, with excellent discipline. There is a standard-bearer there at the bridge. I truly think he is as valiant a man as Mark Antony. He is a man of no rank or consequence, but I saw him fight as gallantly as though he were.

GOWER

What is his name?

FLUELLEN

He is called Ensign Pistol.

GOWER

I don't know him.

PISTOL enters.

FLUELLEN

Here he is.

PISTOL
Captain, I thee beseech to do me favors.
The duke of Exeter doth love thee well.

FLUELLEN
Ay, I praise God, and I have merited some love at his hands.

PISTOL
Bardolph, a soldier firm and sound of heart
And of buxom valor, hath, by cruel Fate
And giddy Fortune's furious fickle wheel,
That goddess blind
That stands upon the rolling restless stone—

FLUELLEN
By your patience, Aunchient Pistol, Fortune is painted blind, with a muffler afore her eyes, to signify to you that Fortune is blind; and she is painted also with a wheel to signify to you, which is the moral of it, that she is turning and inconstant, and mutability and variation; and her foot, look you, is fixed upon a spherical stone, which rolls and rolls and rolls. In good truth, the poet makes a most excellent description of it. Fortune is an excellent moral.

PISTOL
Fortune is Bardolph's foe and frowns on him,
For he hath stolen a pax and hangèd must he be.
A damnèd death!
Let gallows gape for dog, let man go free,
And let not hemp his windpipe suffocate.
But Exeter hath given the doom of death
For pax of little price.
Therefore go speak—the duke will hear thy voice—
And let not Bardolph's vital thread be cut
With edge of penny cord and vile reproach.
Speak, Captain, for his life, and I will thee requite.

FLUELLEN
Aunchient Pistol, I do partly understand your meaning.

PISTOL
Why then, rejoice therefore.

PISTOL

Captain, I have a favor to beg of you. You're on very good terms with the duke of Exeter.

FLUELLEN

Yes, God be praised, I have managed to earn his favor.

PISTOL

Bardolph, a soldier who is loyal and stout-hearted and full of valour, has, by a cruel trick of fate and a turn of silly Fortune's wildly spinning wheel, that blind goddess who stands upon an ever-rolling stone—

FLUELLEN

Now, now, Ensign Pistol. Fortune is depicted as blind, with a scarf over her eyes, to signify that she is blind. And she is depicted with a wheel to signify—this is the point—that she is turning and inconstant, and all about change and variation. And her foot, see, is planted on a spherical stone that rolls and rolls and rolls. Truly, artists do wonderful things with the image of Fortune. She provides an excellent moral.

PISTOL

Pax: a metal tablet bearing a picture of the crucifixion. "Pax" is Latin for "peace," and during the mass, the pax would be kissed by the priest and then by the congregation in a "kiss of peace."

Fortune is Bardolph's enemy. She frowns on him, for he has stolen a pax from a church and he must be hanged. A damnable death! It's fine for dogs to be hung, but men should go free and not have their windpipes strangled with hemp. But Exeter has pronounced a death sentence—and for a cheap little pax. Therefore, go and speak for him! The duke will listen to you. Don't let Bardolph's life be brought to an end by a length of cheap rope and with this shame. Save his life, Captain, and I will repay you.

FLUELLEN

Ensign Pistol, I think I understand you.

PISTOL

I'm glad to hear it.

FLUELLEN

Certainly, auncient, it is not a thing to rejoice at, for if, look you, he were my brother, I would desire the duke to use his good pleasure and put him to execution, for discipline ought to be used.

PISTOL

Die and be damned, and *figo* for thy friendship!

FLUELLEN

It is well.

PISTOL

The fig of Spain!

Exit

FLUELLEN

Very good.

GOWER

Why, this is an arrant counterfeit rascal. I remember him now, a bawd, a cutpurse.

FLUELLEN

I'll assure you, he uttered as prave words at the pridge as you shall see in a summer's day. But it is very well; what he has spoke to me, that is well, I warrant you, when time is serve.

GOWER

Why, 'tis a gull, a fool, a rogue, that now and then goes to the wars to grace himself at his return into London under the form of a soldier. And such fellows are perfect in the great commanders' names, and they will learn you by rote where services were done—at such and such a sconce, at such a breach, at such a convoy; who came off bravely, who was shot, who disgraced, what terms the enemy stood on. And this they con perfectly in the phrase of war, which they

FLUELLEN

Actually, you shouldn't be, because, see, even if he were my own brother I'd want the duke to stick to his plan and have Bardolph executed. Discipline must be kept.

PISTOL

Then die and be damned! And I'm giving the finger to your friendship!

FLUELLEN

Very well.

PISTOL

And the Spanish finger to you!

The "Spanish fig" (also "figo" or "fico") is an obscene hand gesture.

He exits.

FLUELLEN

Very good.

GOWER

Why, that man is a total fraud and rascal. I remember him now. A pimp, a pickpocket.

FLUELLEN

At the bridge he spoke as excellently as anyone I've ever heard, I promise you. But that's alright. What he just said to me—it's alright. I assure you, when the time comes—

GOWER

Why, he's a fool, an idiot, a moron, a man who now and then joins the army so as to be able to give himself airs when he gets back to London and masquerades as a soldier. Such fellows have memorized the names of famous commanders, and they can tell you—having learned such things by rote, not by experience—where this or that battle was fought, at such and such fort, at such and such wall, with such and such protective escort. And they can say who fought well, who trick up with new-tuned oaths; and what a beard of the general's cut and a horrid suit of the camp will do among foaming bottles and ale-washed wits is wonderful to be thought on. But you must learn to know such slanders of the age, or else you may be marvelously mistook.

FLUELLEN
I tell you what, Captain Gower. I do perceive he is not the man that he would gladly make show to the world he is. If I find a hole in his coat, I will tell him my mind.

Drum and colors

Enter KING HENRY, GLOUCESTER, *and soldiers*

Hark you, the king is coming, and I must speak with him from the pridge.—God pless your Majesty.

KING HENRY
How now, Fluellen, cam'st thou from the bridge?

FLUELLEN
Ay, so please your Majesty. The duke of Exeter has very gallantly maintained the pridge. The French is gone off, look you, and there is gallant and most prave passages. Marry, th' athversary was have possession of the pridge, but he is enforced to retire, and the duke of Exeter is master of the pridge. I can tell your Majesty, the duke is a prave man.

KING HENRY
What men have you lost, Fluellen?

FLUELLEN
The perdition of th' athversary hath been very great, reasonable great. Marry, for my part, I think the duke hath lost never a man, but one that is like to be executed for robbing a church, one Bardolph, if your Majesty know the

was shot, who was disgraced, what terms the enemy insisted on. And they study how to express these things in proper military jargon, which they embellish with fashionable oaths. And what a beard trimmed like the general's or a rough uniform will do among foaming mugs and brains washed with ale, you wouldn't believe. But you must learn to recognize such liars, or you will be greatly taken advantage of.

FLUELLEN

I tell you what, Captain Gower; I perceive that he is not the man that he would have the world think he is. If I find an opportunity, I will give him a piece of my mind.

KING HENRY, GLOUCESTER, *and soldiers enter, with a drum roll and military flags.*

Listen. The king is coming, and I must speak with him about what went on at the bridge.—God bless your Majesty!

KING HENRY

Tell me, Fluellen: did you just come from the bridge?

FLUELLEN

Yes, your Majesty. The duke of Exeter has held the bridge very gallantly. The French have retreated, see, and there were great acts of courage. Indeed, the enemy nearly took the bridge, but he was forced to retreat, and the duke of Exeter holds the bridge. I can tell your Majesty, the duke is a brave man.

KING HENRY

What men have you lost, Fluellen?

FLUELLEN

The enemy's losses have been very great, pretty substantial. To tell the truth, though, I think the duke hasn't lost a single man, except for one who will probably be executed for robbing a church, one Barman. His face is all bubukles and whelks and knobs and flames o' fire; and his lips blows at his nose, and it is like a coal of fire, sometimes plue and sometimes red, but his nose is executed, and his fire's out.

KING HENRY
We would have all such offenders so cut off, and we give express charge that in our marches through the country there be nothing compelled from the villages, nothing taken but paid for, none of the French upbraided or abused in disdainful language; for when lenity and cruelty play for a kingdom, the gentler gamester is the soonest winner.

Tucket

Enter MONTJOY

MONTJOY
You know me by my habit.

KING HENRY
Well then, I know thee. What shall I know of thee?

MONTJOY
My master's mind.

KING HENRY
Unfold it.

MONTJOY
Thus says my king: "Say thou to Harry of England, though we seemed dead, we did but sleep. Advantage is a better soldier than rashness. Tell him we could have rebuked him at Harfleur, but that we thought not good to bruise an injury till it were full ripe. Now we speak upon our cue, and our voice is imperial. England shall repent his folly, see his

dolph—I don't know if your Majesty knows the man. His face is all pustules and pockmarks, and pimples and inflammation, and his lips blow up toward his nose, which is like a red-hot coal, sometimes blue, sometimes red. But his nose is dead, and the fire's put out.

KING HENRY

I want all such offenders to be dealt with that way, and I give precise orders that in our progress through the country there shall be nothing seized from the villages, nothing taken that is not paid for, none of the French harassed or abused in disrespectful language. For when mercy and cruelty compete for a kingdom, the gentler player is bound to win.

A trumpet plays. MONTJOY *enters.*

MONTJOY

You know from my clothing who I am.

KING HENRY

Well then, I know who you are. What do you have to tell me?

MONTJOY

My master's decision.

KING HENRY

Go ahead.

MONTJOY

My king says this: "Tell Harry of England: though we appeared dead, we were only asleep. Strategy makes a better soldier than haste. Tell him we could have driven him back at Harfleur but thought it unwise to burst a pustule before it had fully ripened. Now the time is right for us to speak, and we do so with imperial authority. The king of England will regret his foolishness, discover his weakness, and marvel at our restraint. Tell him therefore to consider what ransom weakness, and admire our sufferance. Bid him therefore consider of his ransom, which must proportion the losses we have borne, the subjects we have lost, the disgrace we have digested, which, in weight to reanswer, his pettiness would bow under. For our losses, his exchequer is too poor; for th' effusion of our blood, the muster of his kingdom too faint a number; and for our disgrace, his own person, kneeling at our feet but a weak and worthless satisfaction. To this, add defiance, and tell him, for conclusion, he hath betrayed his followers, whose condemnation is pronounced." So far my king and master; so much my office.

KING HENRY

What is thy name? I know thy quality.

MONTJOY

Montjoy.

KING HENRY

Thou dost thy office fairly. Turn thee back,
And tell thy king I do not seek him now
But could be willing to march on to Calais
Without impeachment, for, to say the sooth,
Though 'tis no wisdom to confess so much
Unto an enemy of craft and vantage,
My people are with sickness much enfeebled,
My numbers lessened, and those few I have
Almost no better than so many French,
Who when they were in health, I tell thee, herald,
I thought upon one pair of English legs
Did march three Frenchmen. Yet, forgive me, God,
That I do brag thus. This your air of France
Hath blown that vice in me. I must repent.
Go therefore, tell thy master: here I am.
My ransom is this frail and worthless trunk,
My army but a weak and sickly guard,
Yet, God before, tell him we will come on
Though France himself and such another neighbor

he can offer as a prisoner of war. It must be commensurate with the losses we have suffered, the subjects we have lost, and the indignity we have endured, for which he is too insignificant to sufficiently pay us back. His coffers are too poor to atone for our losses, his entire kingdom too small to account for the amount of blood we've shed, and the sight of him kneeling at our feet an empty satisfaction compared to the indignity we have put up with. Add defiance to all this and, by way of conclusion, tell him that he has betrayed the men who follow him, whose death sentence has been pronounced." My king and master's message delivered, my task is done.

KING HENRY

What is your name? I know your position.

MONTJOY

Montjoy.

KING HENRY

You do your job well. Go back and tell your king I do not seek an encounter with him now but would be willing to march on to Calais without interference, for—to be honest, though it's probably unwise to confess this to a powerful enemy who has the advantage—my men are considerably weakened by illness, my numbers reduced, and those few men I have almost no better than so many Frenchmen, though when they were in good form, I tell you, herald, I thought three Frenchmen walked on every pair of English legs. But God forgive me for bragging. It's a vice I've picked up since I've been here, and I must get rid of it. Anyway, go tell your master I am here. My ransom is my own fragile, worthless body, my army but a weak and sickly escort. But, before God, tell him we will advance, even if the king of France himself and another foe as strong should stand in our way. *(giving him money)* That's for your trouble, Montjoy. Go tell

Stand in our way. There's for thy labor, Montjoy.
Go bid thy master well advise himself:
If we may pass, we will; if we be hindered,
We shall your tawny ground with your red blood
Discolor. And so, Montjoy, fare you well.
The sum of all our answer is but this:
We would not seek a battle as we are,
Nor, as we are, we say we will not shun it.
So tell your master.

MONTJOY
I shall deliver so. Thanks to your Highness.

Exit

GLOUCESTER
I hope they will not come upon us now.

KING HENRY
We are in God's hand, brother, not in theirs.
March to the bridge. It now draws toward night.
Beyond the river we'll encamp ourselves,
And on tomorrow bid them march away.

Exeunt

your master to consider carefully. If we're allowed to pass, we will. If we're prevented, we'll discolor your golden ground with your red blood. And so, Montjoy, farewell. This is our whole answer: We do not seek a battle nor will we avoid one. Tell your master this.

MONTJOY

I'll deliver the message. I thank your Highness.

He exits.

GLOUCESTER

I hope they don't attack us now.

KING HENRY

We're in God's hands, brother, not in theirs. March to the bridge. Night is approaching. We'll set up camp across the river and continue on tomorrow. Give the order to march.

They all exit.

ACT 3, SCENE 7

Enter the CONSTABLE *of France, the Lord* RAMBURES, ORLÉANS, DAUPHIN, *with others*

CONSTABLE
Tut, I have the best armor of the world. Would it were day!

ORLÉANS
You have an excellent armor, but let my horse have his due.

CONSTABLE
It is the best horse of Europe.

ORLÉANS
Will it never be morning?

DAUPHIN
My lord of Orléans, and my Lord High Constable, you talk of horse and armor?

ORLÉANS
You are as well provided of both as any prince in the world.

DAUPHIN
What a long night is this! I will not change my horse with any that treads but on four pasterns. Çà ha! He bounds from the earth, as if his entrails were hairs, le cheval volant, the Pegasus, qui a les narines de feu. When I bestride him, I soar; I am a hawk; he trots the air. The earth sings when he touches it. The basest horn of his hoof is more musical than the pipe of Hermes.

ORLÉANS
He's of the color of the nutmeg.

DAUPHIN
And of the heat of the ginger. It is a beast for Perseus. He is pure air and fire; and the dull elements of earth and water never appear in him, but only in patient stillness while his rider mounts him. He is indeed a horse, and all other jades you may call beasts.

ACT 3, SCENE 7

The CONSTABLE *of France, Lord* RAMBURES, ORLÉANS, *and the* DAUPHIN *enter, with others.*

CONSTABLE

Nonsense. I have the best armor in the world. I wish it were day!

ORLÉANS

You have wonderful armor, but give my horse his due.

CONSTABLE

It is the best horse in Europe.

ORLÉANS

Will it never be morning?

DAUPHIN

My lord of Orléans, and my lord high Constable, are you talking about horses and armor?

ORLÉANS

You are as well provided in both respects as any prince in the world.

DAUPHIN

What a long night this is! I will not trade my horse for any that walks on four legs. He leaps from the ground as if his insides were light as hairs. He's a flying horse, a Pegasus, breathing fire out of his nostrils. When I sit astride him, I soar, I am a hawk. He trots on air. The earth sings when he touches it. The lowest part of his hoof is more musical than Pan's pipe.

ORLÉANS

He's the color of nutmeg.

DAUPHIN

And hot as ginger. He is an animal worthy of Perseus. He is pure air and fire. The duller elements of earth and water have no part in him, except in the moment of patient stillness when his rider mounts him. He is indeed worthy of the name "horse," and you can call all the rest beasts.

CONSTABLE

Indeed, my lord, it is a most absolute and excellent horse.

DAUPHIN

It is the prince of palfreys. His neigh is like the bidding of a monarch, and his countenance enforces homage.

ORLÉANS

No more, cousin.

DAUPHIN

Nay, the man hath no wit that cannot, from the rising of the lark to the lodging of the lamb, vary deserved praise on my palfrey. It is a theme as fluent as the sea. Turn the sands into eloquent tongues, and my horse is argument for them all. 'Tis a subject for a sovereign to reason on, and for a sovereign's sovereign to ride on, and for the world, familiar to us and unknown, to lay apart their particular functions and wonder at him. I once writ a sonnet in his praise and began thus: "Wonder of nature—"

ORLÉANS

I have heard a sonnet begin so to one's mistress.

DAUPHIN

Then did they imitate that which I composed to my courser, for my horse is my mistress.

ORLÉANS

Your mistress bears well.

DAUPHIN

Me well—which is the prescript praise and perfection of a good and particular mistress.

CONSTABLE

Nay, for methought yesterday your mistress shrewdly shook your back.

DAUPHIN

So perhaps did yours.

CONSTABLE

Indeed, my lord, he is a perfectly wonderful horse.

DAUPHIN

He is the prince of horses. His neigh is like a monarch's command. His face demands respect.

ORLÉANS

Enough, cousin.

DAUPHIN

No, the man who cannot extol the virtues of my horse from dawn to dusk is not particularly clever. It's a subject as worthy of endless discussion as the changing sea. If each grain of sand had a tongue to eulogize, my horse would be a topic for them all. He is a subject for a king to contemplate, and for a king's king to ride on, and for the world at large—both friend and stranger—to stop whatever they are doing and marvel at. I once wrote a sonnet in his praise which began, "Wonder of nature—"

ORLÉANS

I have heard a sonnet to one's mistress that began like that.

DAUPHIN

Then the writer imitated the one I composed to my steed, for my horse is my mistress.

ORLÉANS

Your mistress is a good mount.

DAUPHIN

A good mount for me—and that's the highest praise and very definition of a good mistress, that she belong to one alone.

CONSTABLE

Yes, but yesterday I could have sworn your mistress gave you a bumpy ride.

DAUPHIN

So, perhaps, did yours.

CONSTABLE
Mine was not bridled.

DAUPHIN
Oh, then belike she was old and gentle, and you rode, like a kern of Ireland, your French hose off and in your straight strossers.

CONSTABLE
You have good judgment in horsemanship.

DAUPHIN
Be warned by me, then: they that ride so, and ride not warily, fall into foul bogs. I had rather have my horse to my mistress.

CONSTABLE
I had as lief have my mistress a jade.

DAUPHIN
I tell thee, Constable, my mistress wears his own hair.

CONSTABLE
I could make as true a boast as that if I had a sow to my mistress.

DAUPHIN
"Le chien est retourné à son propre vomissement, et la truie lavée au bourbier." Thou mak'st use of anything.

CONSTABLE
Yet do I not use my horse for my mistress, or any such proverb so little kin to the purpose.

RAMBURES
My Lord Constable, the armor that I saw in your tent tonight, are those stars or suns upon it?

CONSTABLE
Stars, my lord.

DAUPHIN
Some of them will fall tomorrow, I hope.

CONSTABLE

Mine wasn't wearing a bridle.

DAUPHIN

Oh, then I guess she was old and gentle, and you rode barelegged, like an Irish yokel.

CONSTABLE

You're a good judge of horsemanship.

DAUPHIN

Take a tip from me, then. Those who don't take care when they ride often find themselves thrown into a messy situation. I'd rather have my horse than a mistress.

CONSTABLE

I'd prefer to keep my mistress rather than some lame horse.

DAUPHIN

I'll tell you this, Constable, my mistress has his own hair.

CONSTABLE

I could make the same boast even if I had a pig as my mistress.

DAUPHIN

"The dog returns to its own vomit, and the newly washed sow to its mud puddle."
You'd take anything for a mistress.

CONSTABLE

At least I don't have a horse for my mistress—or a saying so beside the point.

RAMBURES

My Lord Constable, are those stars or suns I saw on the armor in your tent tonight?

CONSTABLE

Stars, my lord.

DAUPHIN

I hope some will fall off tomorrow.

CONSTABLE
And yet my sky shall not want.

DAUPHIN
That may be, for you bear a many superfluously, and 'twere more honor some were away.

CONSTABLE
Ev'n as your horse bears your praises—who would trot as well were some of your brags dismounted.

DAUPHIN
Would I were able to load him with his desert! Will it never be day? I will trot tomorrow a mile, and my way shall be paved with English faces.

CONSTABLE
I will not say so, for fear I should be faced out of my way. But I would it were morning, for I would fain be about the ears of the English.

RAMBURES
Who will go to hazard with me for twenty prisoners?

CONSTABLE
You must first go yourself to hazard ere you have them.

CONSTABLE

And yet I'll still have plenty.

DAUPHIN

No doubt, for you wear too many in the first place, and it might be more seemly to make do with fewer.

CONSTABLE

Yes, like your horse, who, staggering under your boasts, would trot more easily if some of them dismounted.

DAUPHIN

I only wish I could load him up with all the praise he deserves! Oh, will it never be day?
I will ride out a mile tomorrow and leave the road paved with the faces of dead Englishmen.

CONSTABLE

I'd say the same thing, but I'm afraid I'd be faced out of my way. But I do wish it were morning, for I long to be mixing it up with the English.

"Faced out of my way" would normally mean "bullied" or "pushed off the road," but the Constable is just making a joke about all the faces in the Dauphin's image.

RAMBURES

Would anyone like to bet twenty prisoners with me?

He's suggesting they play a game of chance, using as stakes the Englishmen they plan to capture the next day.

CONSTABLE

You'll have to take some chances yourself before you catch them.

DAUPHIN
'Tis midnight. I'll go arm myself.

Exit

ORLÉANS
The Dauphin longs for morning.

RAMBURES
He longs to eat the English.

CONSTABLE
I think he will eat all he kills.

ORLÉANS
By the white hand of my lady, he's a gallant prince.

CONSTABLE
Swear by her foot, that she may tread out the oath.

ORLÉANS
He is simply the most active gentleman of France.

CONSTABLE
Doing is activity, and he will still be doing.

ORLÉANS
He never did harm that I heard of.

CONSTABLE
Nor will do none tomorrow. He will keep that good name still.

ORLÉANS
I know him to be valiant.

CONSTABLE
I was told that by one that knows him better than you.

ORLÉANS
What's he?

CONSTABLE
Marry, he told me so himself; and he said he cared not who knew it.

ORLÉANS
He needs not. It is no hidden virtue in him.

DAUPHIN

It's midnight. I'll go put my armor on.

He exits.

ORLÉANS

The Dauphin really wants it to be morning.

RAMBURES

He wants to eat the English.

CONSTABLE

I think he'll eat everyone he kills.

In other words, he won't kill anyone.

ORLÉANS

By my mistress's white hand, he's a gallant prince.

CONSTABLE

Swear by her foot, so she can stamp out the oath.

ORLÉANS

He's definitely the most active gentleman of France.

CONSTABLE

Performing is activity, and he is always doing that.

ORLÉANS

He never did harm that I heard of.

CONSTABLE

And he's not going to do any tomorrow. That part of his reputation will stand.

ORLÉANS

I know him to be valiant.

CONSTABLE

I was told that by one who knows him better than you.

ORLÉANS

Who was that?

CONSTABLE

Why, he told me so himself, and he said he didn't care who knew it.

ORLÉANS

He doesn't have to care. His virtue is not hidden.

CONSTABLE
By my faith, sir, but it is; never anybody saw it but his lackey. 'Tis a hooded valor, and when it appears, it will bate.

ORLÈANS
Ill will never said well.

CONSTABLE
I will cap that proverb with "There is flattery in friendship."

ORLÉANS
And I will take up that with "Give the devil his due."

CONSTABLE
Well placed; there stands your friend for the devil. Have at the very eye of that proverb with "A pox of the devil."

ORLÉANS
You are the better at proverbs, by how much "A fool's bolt is soon shot."

CONSTABLE
You have shot over.

ORLÉANS
'Tis not the first time you were overshot.

Enter **MESSENGER**

MESSENGER
My Lord High Constable, the English lie within fifteen hundred paces of your tents.

CONSTABLE
Who hath measured the ground?

MESSENGER
The Lord Grandpré.

CONSTABLE
A valiant and most expert gentleman.—Would it were day! Alas, poor Harry of England! He longs not for the dawning as we do.

CONSTABLE

Oh, but it is, sir. No one but his valet ever saw it. His courage is hidden, and when it is revealed, it will shrink.

ORLÉANS

Ill will never prompted anything well said.

CONSTABLE

I'll challenge that proverb with one of my own: "There is flattery in friendship."

ORLÉANS

And I'll match that with "Give the devil his due."

CONSTABLE

Very apt! Your friend is equated with the devil. I'll go straight for that proverb with "To hell with the devil."

ORLÉANS

You are better at proverbs than I am by as much as "A fool shoots quickly and overshoots his mark."

CONSTABLE

You have overshot.

ORLÉANS

I've outshot you, and not for the first time.

A **MESSENGER** *enters.*

MESSENGER

My Lord High Constable, the English lie within fifteen hundred paces of your tents.

CONSTABLE

Who measured the ground?

MESSENGER

The Lord Grandpré.

CONSTABLE

A very valiant and knowledgeable gentleman. If only it were day! Poor Harry of England! He doesn't long for the dawn as we do.

ORLÉANS
What a wretched and peevish fellow is this king of England to mope with his fat-brained followers so far out of his knowledge.

CONSTABLE
If the English had any apprehension, they would run away.

ORLÉANS
That they lack, for if their heads had any intellectual armor, they could never wear such heavy head-pieces.

RAMBURES
That island of England breeds very valiant creatures. Their mastiffs are of unmatchable courage.

ORLÉANS
Foolish curs, that run winking into the mouth of a Russian bear and have their heads crushed like rotten apples. You may as well say, that's a valiant flea that dare eat his breakfast on the lip of a lion.

CONSTABLE
Just, just; and the men do sympathize with the mastiffs in robustious and rough coming on, leaving their wits with their wives. And then give them great meals of beef and iron and steel, they will eat like wolves and fight like devils.

ORLÉANS
Ay, but these English are shrewdly out of beef.

CONSTABLE
Then shall we find tomorrow they have only stomachs to eat and none to fight. Now is it time to arm. Come, shall we about it?

ORLÉANS
It is now two o'clock. But, let me see, by ten
We shall have each a hundred Englishmen.

Exeunt

ORLÉANS

What a miserable and obstinate fellow this king of England is, to blunder with his fat-headed followers so far beyond his capacity.

CONSTABLE

If the English had any sense, they would run away.

ORLÉANS

Well, obviously they don't. If there were anything inside their heads, they could never wear such heavy helmets.

RAMBURES

That island of England breeds very valiant creatures. Their hounds are unequaled in courage.

ORLÉANS

Foolish dogs, blindly running straight toward a Russian bear only to have their heads crushed like rotten apples. You might just as well say, "That's a valiant flea that dares to eat its breakfast on the lip of a lion."

CONSTABLE

Yes, exactly. And the men resemble their English hounds in their loud, showy ferocity, too, leaving their brains behind with their wives. Give them hefty meals of beef and iron and steel, and they will eat like wolves and fight like devils.

ORLÉANS

Yes, but these English are seriously short of beef.

CONSTABLE

Then tomorrow we'll find that they feel only like eating, not like fighting. It's time to put our armor on. Shall we get started?

ORLÉANS

It's two o'clock now. But let me see, by ten we shall each have captured a hundred Englishmen.

They all exit.

ACT FOUR

PROLOGUE

Enter CHORUS

CHORUS

Now entertain conjecture of a time
When creeping murmur and the poring dark
Fills the wide vessel of the universe.
From camp to camp, through the foul womb of night,
The hum of either army stilly sounds,
That the fixed sentinels almost receive
The secret whispers of each other's watch.
Fire answers fire, and through their paly flames
Each battle sees the other's umbered face.
Steed threatens steed, in high and boastful neighs
Piercing the night's dull ear; and from the tents
The armorers, accomplishing the knights,
With busy hammers closing rivets up,
Give dreadful note of preparation.
The country cocks do crow, the clocks do toll,
And, the third hour of drowsy morning named,
Proud of their numbers and secure in soul,
The confident and overlusty French
Do the low-rated English play at dice
And chide the cripple, tardy-gaited night,
Who like a foul and ugly witch doth limp
So tediously away. The poor condemnèd English,
Like sacrifices, by their watchful fires
Sit patiently and inly ruminate
The morning's danger; and their gesture sad,
Investing lank-lean cheeks and war-worn coats,
Presenteth them unto the gazing moon
So many horrid ghosts. Oh, now, who will behold
The royal captain of this ruined band

ACT FOUR

PROLOGUE

The CHORUS *enters.*

CHORUS

Now summon up the image of stealthy murmurs and engulfing darkness filling the wide vessel of the universe. From camp to camp through the dark cave of night, the noise from both armies grows so quiet that those standing watch almost think they can hear the whispered secrets of one another's sentinels. One by one, fires are lit on both sides, and through their pale flames, each army thinks he sees the smoke-tinged faces of the other. The horses of each army answer one another's proud, threatening neighs as they pierce the dull night, and from the tents the sound of the blacksmiths' hammers as they fit out the knights, closing rivets up, adds a note of fear to the preparations. The country cocks crow and the clocks toll, sounding a drowsy three o'clock in the morning. Proud of their army and secure in their numbers, the confident and overeager French play dice, betting on how many worthless Englishmen each will capture. They scold the limping, slowly moving night, which, like an ugly old woman, takes so long to pass. The poor doomed English, like sacrificial beasts, sit patiently, and privately contemplate the dangers that will arrive with morning. With their grave faces, emaciated cheeks, and war-torn coats, they seem to the gazing moon like so many horrifying ghosts. Now, whoever spots the royal captain of this ruined army walking from camp to camp, from tent to tent, let him cry "Praise and glory on his head!" For out he goes visiting all his troops. He bids them good morning with a modest

Walking from watch to watch, from tent to tent?
Let him cry, "Praise and glory on his head!"
For forth he goes and visits all his host,
Bids them good morrow with a modest smile,
And calls them brothers, friends, and countrymen.
Upon his royal face there is no note
How dread an army hath enrounded him,
Nor doth he dedicate one jot of color
Unto the weary and all-watchèd night,
But freshly looks and overbears attaint
With cheerful semblance and sweet majesty,
That every wretch, pining and pale before,
Beholding him, plucks comfort from his looks.
A largess universal, like the sun,
His liberal eye doth give to everyone,
Thawing cold fear, that mean and gentle all
Behold, as may unworthiness define,
A little touch of Harry in the night.
And so our scene must to the battle fly,
Where, Oh, for pity, we shall much disgrace,
With four or five most vile and ragged foils
Right ill-disposed in brawl ridiculous,
The name of Agincourt. Yet sit and see,
Minding true things by what their mock'ries be.

Exit

smile and calls them brothers, friends, and countrymen. There is no indication of the mighty army that surrounds them in his expression, nor has the long, sleepless night robbed his face of an ounce of color. Instead, he looks fresh and covers any signs of fatigue with a show of cheerfulness and sweet majesty that every sad and pale wretch takes comfort in when they see him. His generous eye notices everyone, doling out a bounty as far-reaching as the sun, thawing cold fear, so that low and well-born alike may all experience (for want of a better way of putting it) a little touch of Harry in the night. With that, our scene rushes on toward the battle, which we will represent with four or five worn-out fencing foils, a travesty of battle—forgive us!—that disgraces the name of Agincourt. Still, stay to watch, imagining the way it really was from our own inadequate imitation.

The CHORUS *exits.*

ACT 4, SCENE 1

Enter KING HENRY, BEDFORD, *and* GLOUCESTER

KING HENRY

Gloucester, 'tis true that we are in great danger.
The greater therefore should our courage be.
—Good morrow, brother Bedford. God almighty,
There is some soul of goodness in things evil,
Would men observingly distill it out.
For our bad neighbor makes us early stirrers,
Which is both healthful and good husbandry.
Besides, they are our outward consciences
And preachers to us all, admonishing
That we should dress us fairly for our end.
Thus may we gather honey from the weed
And make a moral of the devil himself.

Enter ERPINGHAM

Good morrow, old Sir Thomas Erpingham.
A good soft pillow for that good white head
Were better than a churlish turf of France.

ERPINGHAM

Not so, my liege, this lodging likes me better,
Since I may say, "Now lie I like a king."

KING HENRY

'Tis good for men to love their present pains
Upon example. So the spirit is eased.
And when the mind is quickened, out of doubt,
The organs, though defunct and dead before,
Break up their drowsy grave and newly move,
With casted slough and fresh legerity.
Lend me thy cloak, Sir Thomas. Brothers both,

ACT 4, SCENE 1

KING HENRY *enters with* **BEDFORD** *and* **GLOUCESTER**.

KING HENRY

Gloucester, it's true that we are in great danger. But our courage should only be the greater for that. Good morning, brother Bedford. God Almighty, there must be some essential goodness even in evil, if men would only look for it. In our case, our bad neighbors over their make us early risers, a healthy and sensible thing to be. Besides, they act as outward consciences and preachers to us all, a visible reminder that we should prepare ourselves for death. Think like that, and you'll manage to get honey out of a common weed and find a moral lesson in the devil himself.

ERPINGHAM *enters*.

Good morning, old Sir Thomas Erpingham! A nice, soft pillow would be a more suitable place to lay that good white head than France's hard, cold ground.

ERPINGHAM

Not at all, my liege. I prefer these quarters, since they allow me to say, "Now I live like a king."

KING HENRY

It's good for men to be given an example of how to take pleasure in discomfort. It eases the spirit. And when the mind is engaged, the rest of the body, dead and dull before, wakes up and comes to life with a new nimbleness and sensitivity, like a snake shedding its dead skin. Lend me your cloak, Sir Thomas. Brothers,

Commend me to the princes in our camp,
Do my good morrow to them, and anon
Desire them all to my pavilion.

GLOUCESTER
We shall, my liege.

ERPINGHAM
Shall I attend your Grace?

KING HENRY
No, my good knight.
Go with my brothers to my lords of England.
I and my bosom must debate awhile,
And then I would no other company.

ERPINGHAM
The Lord in heaven bless thee, noble Harry!

Exeunt all but KING HENRY

KING HENRY
God-a-mercy, old heart, thou speak'st cheerfully.

Enter PISTOL

PISTOL
Qui vous là?

KING HENRY
A friend.

PISTOL
Discuss unto me: art thou officer or art thou base, common, and popular?

KING HENRY
I am a gentleman of a company.

PISTOL
Trail'st thou the puissant pike?

KING HENRY
Even so. What are you?

PISTOL
As good a gentleman as the emperor.

give my regards to the princes in our camp. Say good day to them from me and ask them to come to my tent.

GLOUCESTER
We shall, my liege.

ERPINGHAM
Shall I accompany your Grace?

KING HENRY
No, my good knight. Go with my brothers to my English peers. I need to be alone with my thoughts for a while and don't want any company.

ERPINGHAM
The Lord in heaven bless you, noble Harry!

All but KING HENRY *exit.*

KING HENRY
Bless you, old soul! Your words cheer my heart.

PISTOL *enters.*

PISTOL
(*speaking in French*) Who goes there?

KING HENRY
A friend.

PISTOL
Declare yourself to me. Are you an officer? Or are you low, vulgar, and of the common people?

KING HENRY
I am a gentleman of a company.

PISTOL
Do you carry a pike?

KING HENRY
Exactly. What about you?

PISTOL
I'm as good a gentleman as the emperor.

KING HENRY
Then you are a better than the king.

PISTOL
The king's a bawcock, and a heart of gold,
A lad of life, an imp of fame,
Of parents good, of fist most valiant.
I kiss his dirty shoe, and from heartstring
I love the lovely bully. What is thy name?

KING HENRY
Harry le Roy.

PISTOL
Le Roy? A Cornish name. Art thou of Cornish crew?

KING HENRY
No, I am a Welshman.

PISTOL
Know'st thou Fluellen?

KING HENRY
Yes.

PISTOL
Tell him I'll knock his leek about his pate
Upon Saint Davy's day.

KING HENRY
Do not you wear your dagger in your cap that day, lest he knock that about yours.

PISTOL
Art thou his friend?

KING HENRY
And his kinsman too.

PISTOL
The *figo* for thee then!

KING HENRY
I thank you. God be with you.

PISTOL
My name is Pistol called.

Exit

KING HENRY
Then you're a better man than the king.

PISTOL
The king's a dear boy with a heart of gold, he's a lively lad, a wag, born of fine parents, good with his fists. I kiss his dirty shoe, and from the bottom of my heart I love the lovely boy. What is your name?

KING HENRY
Harry le Roy.

PISTOL
Le Roy? That's a Cornish name. Are you with a Cornish company?

KING HENRY
No, I am a Welshman.

PISTOL
Do you know Fluellen?

KING HENRY
Yes.

PISTOL
Tell him I'll take the leek out of his hat on Saint Davy's Day and slap his head with it.

KING HENRY
You'd better not wear your dagger in your cap that day, or he might slap your head with it.

PISTOL
Are you his friend?

KING HENRY
Yes, and his relative, too.

PISTOL
Then I'm giving you the finger.

KING HENRY
Thank you. God be with you.

PISTOL
My name is Pistol.

He exits.

KING HENRY
It sorts well with your fierceness.

Enter FLUELLEN *and* GOWER

GOWER
Captain Fluellen.

FLUELLEN
So. In the name of Jesu Christ, speak fewer. It is the greatest admiration in the universal world when the true and aunchient prerogatifes and laws of the wars is not kept. If you would take the pains but to examine the wars of Pompey the Great, you shall find, I warrant you, that there is no tiddle toddle nor pibble babble in Pompey's camp. I warrant you, you shall find the ceremonies of the wars and the cares of it and the forms of it and the sobriety of it and the modesty of it to be otherwise.

GOWER
Why, the enemy is loud. You hear him all night.

FLUELLEN
If the enemy is an ass and a fool and a prating coxcomb, is it meet, think you, that we should also, look you, be an ass and a fool and a prating coxcomb, in your own conscience, now?

GOWER
I will speak lower.

FLUELLEN
I pray you and beseech you that you will.

Exeunt GOWER *and* FLUELLEN

KING HENRY
Though it appear a little out of fashion,
There is much care and valor in this Welshman.

Enter three soldiers, John BATES, *Alexander* COURT, *and Michael* WILLIAMS

KING HENRY
The name suits your fierceness.

FLUELLEN and GOWER enter.

GOWER
Captain Fluellen!

FLUELLEN
In the name of Jesus Christ, keep it down! It never ceases to amaze me the way people ignore the correct, traditional principles and rules of war. If you would take the trouble to study the tactics of Pompey the Great, I can tell you that you would find no tittle-tattle or pibble-pabble in Pompey's camp. I tell you, you would find the rituals of war and, I promise you, its ceremonies and its solicitudes and its forms and its gravity and its discipline all to be quite counter to all this noise.

GOWER
But the enemy is loud. You can hear them all night long.

FLUELLEN
And if the enemy is an ass and a fool and a prating idiot, does that mean, you think, that we should also be an ass and a fool and a prating idiot? Think about it.

GOWER
I will lower my voice.

FLUELLEN
I'd be very glad if you would.

GOWER and FLUELLEN exit.

KING HENRY
Though he seems a little old-fashioned, there is much care and courage in this Welshman.

Three soldiers, John BATES, Alexander COURT, and Michael WILLIAMS, enter.

COURT

Brother John Bates, is not that the morning which breaks yonder?

BATES

I think it be, but we have no great cause to desire the approach of day.

WILLIAMS

We see yonder the beginning of the day, but I think we shall never see the end of it.—Who goes there?

KING HENRY

A friend.

WILLIAMS

Under what captain serve you?

KING HENRY

Under Sir Thomas Erpingham.

WILLIAMS

A good old commander and a most kind gentleman. I pray you, what thinks he of our estate?

KING HENRY

Even as men wracked upon a sand, that look to be washed off the next tide.

BATES

He hath not told his thought to the king?

KING HENRY

No. Nor it is not meet he should, for, though I speak it to you, I think the king is but a man as I am. The violet smells to him as it doth to me. The element shows to him as it doth to me. All his senses have but human conditions. His ceremonies laid by, in his nakedness he appears but a man, and though his affections are higher mounted than ours, yet when they stoop, they stoop with the like wing. Therefore, when he sees reason of fears as we do, his fears, out of doubt, be of the same relish as ours are. Yet, in reason, no man should possess him with any appearance of fear, lest he, by showing it, should dishearten his army.

COURT

Brother John Bates, isn't that dawn breaking over there?

BATES

I think it is. But we have no great reason to long for day.

WILLIAMS

That's the beginning of the day we see, but I don't think we'll see the end of it.—Who goes there?

KING HENRY

A friend.

WILLIAMS

What captain do you serve?

KING HENRY

Sir Thomas Erpingham.

WILLIAMS

A veteran commander and a very kind gentleman. Tell me, what does he think of our situation?

KING HENRY

We're men beached on the sand, hoping to be washed out by the next tide.

BATES

He hasn't told this to the king, has he?

KING HENRY

No, nor would it be right for him to. Though it's not my place to say so, I think the king is, after all, only a man, the same as me. The violet smells to him the same as it does to me. The sky appears to him much as it does to me, and all his senses are those of a mortal man. Without his fine clothes, the king appears just like any other naked man. And though his feelings may be pitched higher than ours, when they plummet, they plummet that much farther. Therefore, when he has reason to fear, as we do, his fears are without question of the same order. Still, it stands to reason that he mustn't betray his fear, as it might dishearten his army.

BATES

He may show what outward courage he will, but I believe, as cold a night as 'tis, he could wish himself in Thames up to the neck; and so I would he were, and I by him, at all adventures, so we were quit here.

KING HENRY

By my troth, I will speak my conscience of the king. I think he would not wish himself anywhere but where he is.

BATES

Then I would he were here alone; so should he be sure to be ransomed, and a many poor men's lives saved.

KING HENRY

I dare say you love him not so ill to wish him here alone, howsoever you speak this to feel other men's minds. Methinks I could not die anywhere so contented as in the king's company, his cause being just and his quarrel honorable.

WILLIAMS

That's more than we know.

BATES

Ay, or more than we should seek after, for we know enough if we know we are the king's subjects. If his cause be wrong, our obedience to the king wipes the crime of it out of us.

WILLIAMS

But if the cause be not good, the king himself hath a heavy reckoning to make, when all those legs and arms and heads, chopped off in a battle, shall join together at the latter day, and cry all, "We died at such a place," some swearing, some crying for a surgeon, some upon their wives left poor behind them, some upon the debts they owe, some upon their children rawly left. I am afeard there are few die well that die in a battle, for how can they charitably dispose of

BATES

He can act as brave as he wants, but I believe on a cold night like this he wishes he were neck-deep in the Thames, and I wish he were, too, and I with him, whatever the danger, so long as we were far away from here.

KING HENRY

I'll tell you truly what I think about the king in my heart. I don't think he wants to be anywhere but where he is.

BATES

Then I wish he were here alone. He'd be sure to be ransomed, and many a poor man's life saved.

KING HENRY

Oh, I'm sure you don't dislike him so much as to wish he were here alone, even though you say this to find out how the rest of us feel. I don't think there's anywhere I'd rather die than in the king's company, as his cause is just and honorable.

WILLIAMS

That's more than we know.

BATES

Yes, and more than we should seek to know. It's enough that we know we're the king's subjects. If his cause is wrong, our obedience to the king clears us of responsibility for it.

WILLIAMS

But if the cause is not just, the king himself will have a lot to answer for, when all those legs and arms and heads chopped off in battle shall join together on Judgment Day crying, "We died at such and such a place." Some will be swearing, some crying for a surgeon, some for the wives that are destitute without them, some about the debts they owed, some for their children left unprovided for. I think few die well who anything, when blood is their argument? Now, if these men do not die well, it will be a black matter for the king that led them to it, who to disobey were against all proportion of subjection.

KING HENRY

So, if a son that is by his father sent about merchandise do sinfully miscarry upon the sea, the imputation of his wickedness, by your rule, should be imposed upon his father that sent him. Or if a servant, under his master's command transporting a sum of money, be assailed by robbers and die in many irreconciled iniquities, you may call the business of the master the author of the servant's damnation. But this is not so. The king is not bound to answer the particular endings of his soldiers, the father of his son, nor the master of his servant, for they purpose not their death, when they purpose their services. Besides, there is no king, be his cause never so spotless, if it come to the arbitrament of swords, can try it out with all unspotted soldiers. Some, peradventure, have on them the guilt of premeditated and contrived murder; some, of beguiling virgins with the broken seals of perjury; some, making the wars their bulwark, that have before gored the gentle bosom of peace with pillage and robbery. Now, if these men have defeated the law and outrun native punishment, though they can outstrip men, they have no wings to fly from God. War is His beadle, war is His vengeance, so that here men are punished for before-breach of the king's laws in now the king's quarrel. Where they feared the death, they have borne life away; and where they would be safe, they perish. Then, if they die unprovided, no more is the king guilty of their damnation than he was before guilty of those impieties for the which they are now visited. Every subject's duty is the king's, but every subject's soul is his own. Therefore should every soldier in the wars do as every sick man in his bed: wash every mote out of his conscience. And, dying so, death is to him advantage; or not dying, the die in battle. How can a person expect to resolve anything in a Christian manner when they've passed their lives killing? Now, if these men don't die in a state of grace, it will be a heavy charge against the king who led them into battle, whom they, as his subjects, could not disobey.

KING HENRY

The king isn't responsible for the particular end each soldier comes to, nor is the father responsible for his son's final end or the master for his servant's. The father and the master and the king didn't order their subordinates' deaths when they ordered their services. Besides, there's no king, however pure his cause, who, if it comes to a trial by combat, can rely on using completely blameless soldiers. Perhaps some may be guilty of plotting murder, some of seducing maidens with lies and then abandoning them; some, of looting and stealing before they were even hired as soldiers. Even if these men have escaped the law and punishment at home, they cannot escape God. War is God's agent of justice. War is vengeance. So there are men here who have broken the king's law earlier and are punished now in his war. When they feared death, they escaped with their lives; and now where they imagine they're safe, they perish. So, if they die unprepared, the king is no more guilty of their damnation than he was guilty of the earlier crimes they're finally being punished for. Every subject's duty is the king's, but every subject's soul is his own. Therefore, every soldier should do as any man who is sick in his bed would do: clear his conscience of any stain. Then if he dies, his death serves him. Or, if he doesn't die, the time he spent preparing himself was at least blessed. And in the case of the man who survives, one could be forgiven for supposing that God spared him exactly because he was so ready to die; now he can live

time was blessedly lost wherein such preparation was gained. And in him that escapes, it were not sin to think that, making God so free an offer, He let him outlive that day to see His greatness and to teach others how they should prepare.

WILLIAMS

'Tis certain, every man that dies ill, the ill upon his own head. The king is not to answer it.

BATES

I do not desire he should answer for me, and yet I determine to fight lustily for him.

KING HENRY

I myself heard the king say he would not be ransomed.

WILLIAMS

Ay, he said so, to make us fight cheerfully, but when our throats are cut, he may be ransomed, and we ne'er the wiser.

KING HENRY

If I live to see it, I will never trust his word after.

WILLIAMS

You pay him then. That's a perilous shot out of an elder gun, that a poor and private displeasure can do against a monarch. You may as well go about to turn the sun to ice with fanning in his face with a peacock's feather. You'll "never trust his word after." Come, 'tis a foolish saying.

KING HENRY

Your reproof is something too round. I should be angry with you if the time were convenient.

WILLIAMS

Let it be a quarrel between us, if you live.

to appreciate God's greatness and teach others to prepare.By this reasoning, if a son is sent by his father on business and drowns at sea while still in a state of sin, his wickedness is his father's fault. Or if a servant, carrying a sum of money for his master, is attacked by robbers and dies without confessing his sins, we can say that the master's business is to blame for the servant's damnation. But that isn't so.

WILLIAMS

It's clear, every man must take responsibility for the manner of his own death. The king is not responsible for it.

BATES

I don't expect him to answer for me, and yet I'm determined to fight vigorously for him.

KING HENRY

I myself heard the king say he would not be ransomed.

WILLIAMS

Sure, he said so to make us fight cheerfully. But when our throats are cut, he could be ransomed without our being any the wiser.

KING HENRY

If I live to see it, I'll never trust his word again.

WILLIAMS

Yeah, right, go get him. That's a lame threat from a toy gun, a poor individual's private displeasure with a monarch. You may as well try to turn the sun to ice by fanning its face with a peacock feather. You'll "never trust his word again." Come on, that was a stupid thing to say.

KING HENRY

Your scolding is somewhat overblown. I'd be angry with you if the occasion allowed.

WILLIAMS

Let it be a quarrel between us, if you live.

KING HENRY
I embrace it.

WILLIAMS
How shall I know thee again?

KING HENRY
Give me any gage of thine, and I will wear it in my bonnet. Then, if ever thou dar'st acknowledge it, I will make it my quarrel.

WILLIAMS
Here's my glove. Give me another of thine.

KING HENRY
There.

WILLIAMS
This will I also wear in my cap. If ever thou come to me and say, after tomorrow, "This is my glove," by this hand I will take thee a box on the ear.

KING HENRY
If ever I live to see it, I will challenge it.

WILLIAMS
Thou dar'st as well be hanged.

KING HENRY
Well, I will do it, though I take thee in the king's company.

WILLIAMS
Keep thy word. Fare thee well.

BATES
Be friends, you English fools, be friends. We have French quarrels enough, if you could tell how to reckon.

KING HENRY
Indeed, the French may lay twenty French crowns to one they will beat us, for they bear them on their shoulders. But it is no English treason to cut French crowns, and tomorrow the king himself will be a clipper.

KING HENRY
I'm game.

WILLIAMS
How will I recognize you in the future?

KING HENRY
Give me some trinket of yours, and I will wear it in my hat. Then, if you dare to acknowledge it, I'll take up my quarrel with you.

WILLIAMS
Here's my glove; give me one of yours.

KING HENRY
Here.

WILLIAMS
I'll also wear this in my cap. If you come to me after tomorrow and say, "That's my glove," I swear by this hand, I will take it and give you a box on the ear.

KING HENRY
If I ever see it, I will challenge you.

WILLIAMS
You may as well undertake to be hanged.

KING HENRY
I'll do it even if I find you in the company of the king himself.

WILLIAMS
Keep your word. Farewell.

BATES
Be friends, you English fools, be friends: we have enough enemies on the French side, if either of you could count.

KING HENRY
Indeed, the French can bet twenty French crowns to one that they'll beat us, they have such an army. But it's no treason for an Englishman to cut off a French crown—a head, I mean—and tomorrow the king himself will do some snipping.

Exeunt soldiers

Upon the king! Let us our lives, our souls, our debts, our careful wives, our children, and our sins lay on the king!
We must bear all. O hard condition,
Twin-born with greatness, subject to the breath
Of every fool, whose sense no more can feel
But his own wringing. What infinite heart's ease
Must kings neglect that private men enjoy?
And what have kings that privates have not too,
Save ceremony, save general ceremony?
And what art thou, thou idol ceremony?
What kind of god art thou, that suffer'st more
Of mortal griefs than do thy worshippers?
What are thy rents? What are thy comings in?
O ceremony, show me but thy worth!
What is thy soul of adoration?
Art thou aught else but place, degree, and form,
Creating awe and fear in other men,
Wherein thou art less happy, being feared,
Than they in fearing?
What drink'st thou oft, instead of homage sweet,
But poisoned flattery? Oh, be sick, great greatness,
And bid thy ceremony give thee cure!
Think'st thou the fiery fever will go out
With titles blown from adulation?
Will it give place to flexure and low bending?
Canst thou, when thou command'st the beggar's knee,
Command the health of it? No, thou proud dream,
That play'st so subtly with a king's repose.
I am a king that find thee, and I know
'Tis not the balm, the scepter, and the ball,
The sword, the mace, the crown imperial,
The intertissued robe of gold and pearl,
The farcèd title running 'fore the king,
The throne he sits on, nor the tide of pomp

BATES, **COURT**, *and* **WILLIAMS** *exit*.

Upon the king! "Let's lay everything upon the king: our lives, our souls, our debts, our anxious wives, our children, and our sins." I must bear responsibility for all of it. What a painful condition responsibility is. It goes along with being born to greatness, but it makes you get badmouthed by every fool who only has his own suffering to care about. What infinite peace do king's give up that private men enjoy? What do kings have that private men do not, besides the pomp of their position? And what is this useless ceremony of kings? What kind of god is ceremony, which suffers more than its worshippers do? What income, what profit does it bring in? Oh, ceremony, only show me your value! Why are you adored? Do you amount to anything besides position, status, and ritual, which inspire awe and fear in others? You're less happy, being feared, than they are in fearing you. What do you get to drink, instead of sweet obedience, but poisonous flattery? Try being sick, great greatness, and see if ceremony can cure you! Do you think fiery fever can be put out by the windy puff of titles? Will it be chased away by bowing and scraping? You can command a beggar to bow on bended knee, but can you take possession of his health? No, vain illusion, so intricately bound up with a king's rest. I who understand you, gorgeous ceremony, because I'm a king and I know that neither the balm, the scepter, and the ball, the robe layered in gold and pearls, the fancy title that precedes the king, the throne he sits on, nor the tide of pomp that beats upon the high shore of this world—not all of these put together, not all of these laid down at night in an imperial bed, can cause the king to rest so soundly as does the miserable wretch who turns in at night with a full stomach and an empty mind, fed on

The outward symbols of kingship

That beats upon the high shore of this world.
No, not all these, thrice-gorgeous ceremony,
Not all these, laid in bed majestical,
Can sleep so soundly as the wretched slave,
Who, with a body filled and vacant mind,
Gets him to rest, crammed with distressful bread;
Never sees horrid night, the child of hell,
But, like a lackey, from the rise to set
Sweats in the eye of Phoebus, and all night
Sleeps in Elysium; next day after dawn,
Doth rise and help Hyperion to his horse,
And follows so the ever-running year
With profitable labor to his grave.
And, but for ceremony, such a wretch,
Winding up days with toil and nights with sleep,
Had the forehand and vantage of a king.
The slave, a member of the country's peace,
Enjoys it, but in gross brain little wots
What watch the king keeps to maintain the peace,
Whose hours the peasant best advantages.

Enter ERPINGHAM

ERPINGHAM
My lord, your nobles, jealous of your absence,
Seek through your camp to find you.

KING HENRY
Good old knight,
Collect them all together at my tent.
I'll be before thee.

ERPINGHAM
I shall do't, my lord.

Exit

the bread of his daily struggle. He never wakes to horrifying darkness, born of hell, but sweats in the hot sun from dawn to dusk and all night long sleeps in peace. Come morning, he wakes and helps the sun into his chariot and so wears out the ever-rolling years until his death. Apart from ceremony, this poor creature who spends his days in toil and his nights in sleep is better off than the king. The peasant enjoys his country's peace without ever worrying his dull head about the vigil the king must keep to maintain that peace.

ERPINGHAM *enters.*

ERPINGHAM
My lord, your noble subjects are looking for you all over the camp. They're anxious to see you.

KING HENRY
Good old knight, gather them all together at my tent. I'll meet you there.

ERPINGHAM
Consider it done, my lord.

He exits.

KING HENRY

O God of battles, steel my soldiers' hearts.
Possess them not with fear. Take from them now
The sense of reck'ning ere th' opposèd numbers
Pluck their hearts from them. Not today, O Lord,
Oh, not today, think not upon the fault
My father made in compassing the crown.
I Richard's body have interrèd anew,
And on it have bestowed more contrite tears
Than from it issued forcèd drops of blood.
Five hundred poor I have in yearly pay,
Who twice a day their withered hands hold up
Toward heaven to pardon blood. And I have built
Two chantries where the sad and solemn priests
Sing still for Richard's soul. More will I do—
Though all that I can do is nothing worth,
Since that my penitence comes after all,
Imploring pardon.

Enter GLOUCESTER

GLOUCESTER

My liege.

KING HENRY

My brother Gloucester's voice.—Ay,
I know thy errand. I will go with thee.
The day, my friends, and all things stay for me.

Exeunt

KING HENRY

Oh God of battles, bolster my soldiers' courage. Don't let them know fear. Rob them of the ability to count before the numbers against them overwhelm their courage. And just for today, Oh, Lord, just today don't think of the crime my father committed in seizing the crown! I've transferred Richard's body to a new grave and on it poured more tears of remorse than it has shed drops of blood. I've hired five hundred almsmen to hold up their withered hands to heaven, praying for my pardon twice a day throughout the year. And I've built two chapels where solemn priests sing continually for Richard's soul. I will do more, though nothing I can do is any good since this remorse comes after the crime, asking for pardon.

GLOUCESTER *enters.*

GLOUCESTER

My liege.

KING HENRY

My brother Gloucester's voice? Yes, I know why you've come. I'll go with you. The day, my friends, and everything await me.

They exit.

ACT 4, SCENE 2

Enter the DAUPHIN, ORLÉANS, RAMBURES, *and others*

ORLÉANS
The sun doth gild our armor. Up, my lords.

DAUPHIN
Montez à cheval! My horse, varlet! Lackey! Ha!

ORLÉANS
O brave spirit!

DAUPHIN
Via les eaux et la terre.

ORLÉANS
Rien puis? L'air et feu?

DAUPHIN
Cieux, cousin Orléans.

Enter CONSTABLE

Now, my Lord Constable?

CONSTABLE
Hark how our steeds for present service neigh.

DAUPHIN
Mount them and make incision in their hides,
That their hot blood may spin in English eyes
And dout them with superfluous courage. Ha!

RAMBURES
What, will you have them weep our horses' blood?
How shall we then behold their natural tears?

Enter MESSENGER

ACT 4, SCENE 2

The DAUPHIN *enters with* ORLÉANS, RAMBURES, *and others.*

ORLÉANS

The sun glints off our armor. Awake, my lords!

DAUPHIN

Mount up our horses! Bring my horse, lackey! Ha!

ORLÉANS

Oh, brave spirit!

DAUPHIN

He'll take me through flood and field.

ORLÉANS

Is that all? How about air and fire?

DAUPHIN

Just the heavens, cousin Orléans.

The CONSTABLE *enters.*

Is it time, my Lord Constable?

CONSTABLE

Listen to our horses neighing, longing to be working.

DAUPHIN

Mount them and dig your spurs into their flanks so that their hot blood may spurt in English eyes and douse them with some of the spare courage we have around. Ha!

RAMBURES

What, you want them to weep our horses' blood? Then how will we see their own natural tears?

A MESSENGER *enters.*

MESSENGER
The English are embattled, you French peers.

CONSTABLE
To horse, you gallant princes, straight to horse.
Do but behold yond poor and starvèd band,
And your fair show shall suck away their souls,
Leaving them but the shales and husks of men.
There is not work enough for all our hands,
Scarce blood enough in all their sickly veins
To give each naked curtal axe a stain,
That our French gallants shall today draw out
And sheathe for lack of sport. Let us but blow on them,
The vapor of our valor will o'erturn them.
'Tis positive against all exceptions, lords,
That our superfluous lackeys and our peasants,
Who in unnecessary action swarm
About our squares of battle, were enough
To purge this field of such a hilding foe,
Though we upon this mountain's basis by
Took stand for idle speculation,
But that our honors must not. What's to say?
A very little little let us do,
And all is done. Then let the trumpets sound
The tucket sonance and the note to mount,
For our approach shall so much dare the field
That England shall couch down in fear and yield.

Enter GRANDPRÉ

GRANDPRÉ
Why do you stay so long, my lords of France?
Yond island carrions, desperate of their bones,
Ill-favoredly become the morning field.
Their ragged curtains poorly are let loose,
And our air shakes them passing scornfully.
Big Mars seems bankrupt in their beggared host
And faintly through a rusty beaver peeps.

MESSENGER

The English are in the field, French lords.

CONSTABLE

To our horses, you gallant princes. Let's mount straight away. All we have to do is look at that poor starving army, and our wonderful display of strength will eat away their souls, leaving them the mere husk of men. There isn't enough work out there to keep us all busy, and hardly enough blood in all their sickly veins put together to put a stain on each of our swords, which our French knights will take out and then put away again, with nothing to do. Let's blow on them. The breath of our valor will send them sprawling. There's no question, lords, but that those extra servants and peasants swarming uselessly around our battle formations would be sufficient to rid this field of such a good-for-nothing foe, while we ourselves stood at the base of this mountain idly looking on. But our honor wouldn't stand for that. What's there to say? Doing the very least will do the whole job. Let the trumpets sound the signal to mount up and march. Our advance will so dazzle the enemy that England will cower in fear and surrender.

GRANDPRÉ *enters.*

GRANDPRÉ

What are you waiting for, lords of France? Those island-bred skeletons, terrified for their bones, are an offensive sight on the morning field. Their ragged banners hang in shreds and the very air of France makes them shiver as it blows by. The god of war looks like a pathetic bankrupt in this miserable army, peeking timidly through a rusty visor. The horsemen stand

The horsemen sit like fixèd candlesticks
With torch staves in their hand, and their poor jades
Lob down their heads, dropping the hides and hips,
The gum down-roping from their pale-dead eyes,
And in their pale dull mouths the gemeled bit
Lies foul with chawed grass, still and motionless.
And their executors, the knavish crows,
Fly o'er them all, impatient for their hour.
Description cannot suit itself in words
To demonstrate the life of such a battle
In life so lifeless, as it shows itself.

CONSTABLE
They have said their prayers, and they stay for death.

DAUPHIN
Shall we go send them dinners and fresh suits,
And give their fasting horses provender,
And after fight with them?

CONSTABLE
I stay but for my guard. On, to the field!
I will the banner from a trumpet take
And use it for my haste. Come, come away.
The sun is high, and we outwear the day.

Exeunt

frozen like candlesticks, torches in their hands. The poor horses droop their heads, their flanks and hips sagging, pus seeping from eyes as pale as death, and in their colorless mouths, the motionless bit is smeared with chewed grass. Meanwhile, their executors, malicious crows, fly over them, impatient for their moment. It's beyond the power of words to describe an army so bereft of life.

Executors: people who dispose of whatever the dead leave behind

CONSTABLE

They've said their prayers, and now they wait for death.

DAUPHIN

Shall we go send them food and fresh clothing and feed their starving horses before we fight them?

CONSTABLE

I'm just waiting for my flag-bearer. But, never mind, I can't wait. To the field! I'll take the banner from a trumpeter and use that. Come, let's be off! The sun is up and we're wasting the day!

They all exit.

ACT 4, SCENE 3

Enter GLOUCESTER, BEDFORD, EXETER, ERPINGHAM, *with all his host,* SALISBURY, *and* WESTMORELAND

GLOUCESTER
Where is the king?

BEDFORD
The king himself is rode to view their battle.

WESTMORELAND
Of fighting men they have full threescore thousand.

EXETER
There's five to one. Besides, they all are fresh.

SALISBURY
God's arm strike with us! 'Tis a fearful odds.
God be wi' you, princes all. I'll to my charge.
If we no more meet till we meet in heaven,
Then joyfully, my noble Lord of Bedford,
My dear Lord Gloucester, and my good Lord Exeter,
And my kind kinsman, warriors all, adieu.

BEDFORD
Farewell, good Salisbury, and good luck go with thee.

EXETER
Farewell, kind lord. Fight valiantly today.
And yet I do thee wrong to mind thee of it,
For thou art framed of the firm truth of valor.

Exit SALISBURY

BEDFORD
He is as full of valor as of kindness,
Princely in both.

Enter KING HENRY

ACT 4, SCENE 3

GLOUCESTER, **BEDFORD**, **EXETER**, **ERPINGHAM**, *with his troops*, **SALISBURY**, *and* **WESTMORELAND** *enter.*

GLOUCESTER
Where is the king?

BEDFORD
The king rode out alone to view their troops.

WESTMORELAND
They have fully sixty thousand fighting men.

EXETER
That's five to one. Besides, they're fresh.

SALISBURY
May God's arm strike on our side! These are frightening odds. God be with all of you, princes. I'll go and join my men. If we don't meet again before we meet in heaven, still we'll meet joyfully. My noble Lord of Bedford, my dear Lord Gloucester, and my good Lord Exeter, and my kind kinsmen, warriors all, adieu.

BEDFORD
Farewell, good Salisbury; and may good luck go with you.

EXETER
Farewell, kind lord. Fight valiantly today. But then I do you wrong to say as much, since you are the very embodiment of bravery.

SALISBURY *exits.*

BEDFORD
He is as full of courage as of kindness, princely in both.

KING HENRY *enters.*

WESTMORELAND

Oh, that we now had here
But one ten thousand of those men in England
That do no work today.

KING HENRY

What's he that wishes so?
My cousin Westmoreland? No, my fair cousin.
If we are marked to die, we are enough
To do our country loss; and if to live,
The fewer men, the greater share of honor.
God's will, I pray thee wish not one man more.
By Jove, I am not covetous for gold
Nor care I who doth feed upon my cost;
It yearns me not if men my garments wear;
Such outward things dwell not in my desires.
But if it be a sin to covet honor,
I am the most offending soul alive.
No, faith, my coz, wish not a man from England.
God's peace, I would not lose so great an honor
As one man more, methinks, would share from me,
For the best hope I have. Oh, do not wish one more!
Rather proclaim it, Westmoreland, through my host,
That he which hath no stomach to this fight,
Let him depart. His passport shall be made,
And crowns for convoy put into his purse.
We would not die in that man's company
That fears his fellowship to die with us.
This day is called the feast of Crispian.
He that outlives this day and comes safe home,
Will stand o' tiptoe when the day is named
And rouse him at the name of Crispian.
He that shall see this day, and live old age,
Will yearly on the vigil feast his neighbors
And say, "Tomorrow is Saint Crispian."
Then will he strip his sleeve and show his scars,
And say, "These wounds I had on Crispin's day."

WESTMORELAND

Oh, if only we had with us here ten thousand of those men back home in England who aren't working today.

KING HENRY

Who wishes that? My cousin Westmoreland? No, my dear cousin. If we are slated to die, the fewer, the better for our country, and if we're slated to live, the fewer men, the greater the share of honor for each of us. In God's name, I beg you not to wish for one more man. By God, I am not selfish when it comes to money: I don't care who eats at my expense. It doesn't bother me when people borrow my clothing—I don't care about these concrete things. But if it is a sin to be selfish about honor, I am the most guilty soul alive. No, my cousin, don't wish that even one man who is now in England were here instead. By God, I wouldn't lose as much honor as a single man more would cost me, I think—not even if it meant giving up my best hope for victory. Oh, do not wish one more! Instead, make this known throughout the army: whoever has no spirit for this fight, let him depart. He will be given safe conduct and money for his passage home. We would not want to die in the company of a man who fears to die with us. This day is called the Feast of Saint Crispian: he who lives to see this day out and comes home safe will stand tall when this day is named and raise himself up at the mention of Crispian. He who survives this day and lives to see old age shall yearly entertain his neighbors on the eve, saying, "Tomorrow is Saint Crispin's Day." He'll roll up his sleeve and show his scars, saying, "I got these wounds on St. Crispin's Day." Old men forget. But these men will remember every detail of what they did today long after they've forgotten everything else. And as the wine flows, our names, familiar as household words, will be invoked

There are actually two different saints honored on this day—Crispin and Crispian. Henry switches back and forth between them in his speech.

Old men forget; yet all shall be forgot
But he'll remember with advantages
What feats he did that day. Then shall our names,
Familiar in his mouth as household words,
Harry the King, Bedford and Exeter,
Warwick and Talbot, Salisbury and Gloucester,
Be in their flowing cups freshly remembered.
This story shall the good man teach his son,
And Crispin Crispian shall ne'er go by,
From this day to the ending of the world,
But we in it shall be rememberèd—
We few, we happy few, we band of brothers;
For he today that sheds his blood with me
Shall be my brother; be he ne'er so vile,
This day shall gentle his condition;
And gentlemen in England now abed
Shall think themselves accursed they were not here,
And hold their manhoods cheap whiles any speaks
That fought with us upon Saint Crispin's day.

Enter SALISBURY

SALISBURY
My sovereign lord, bestow yourself with speed.
The French are bravely in their battles set,
And will with all expedience charge on us.

KING HENRY
All things are ready if our minds be so.

WESTMORELAND
Perish the man whose mind is backward now!

KING HENRY
Thou dost not wish more help from England, coz?

WESTMORELAND
God's will, my liege, would you and I alone,
Without more help, could fight this royal battle!

again: Harry the King, Bedford and Exeter, Warwick and Talbot, Salisbury and Gloucester. Good men will tell their sons this story and the Feast of St. Crispin will never go by, from this day to the end of time, without our being remembered: we few, we happy few, we band of brothers—for whoever sheds his blood with me today shall be my brother. However humble his birth, this day shall grant him nobility. And men back in English now safe in their beds will curse themselves for not having been here, and think less of their own manhood when they listen to the stories of those who fought with us here on St. Crispin's Day.

SALISBURY *enters.*

SALISBURY

My sovereign lord, join us quickly: the French are all arrayed in battle formation and will charge us at any moment.

KING HENRY

We're ready if our minds are ready.

WESTMORELAND

Let any man perish who isn't ready now!

KING HENRY

You don't wish we had more help from England anymore, cousin?

WESTMORELAND

God Almighty, my liege, I wish that you and I could fight this royal battle all alone.

KING HENRY
Why, now thou hast unwished five thousand men,
Which likes me better than to wish us one.
—You know your places. God be with you all.
Tucket

Enter MONTJOY

MONTJOY
Once more I come to know of thee, King Harry,
If for thy ransom thou wilt now compound,
Before thy most assurèd overthrow.
For certainly thou art so near the gulf
Thou needs must be englutted. Besides, in mercy,
The constable desires thee thou wilt mind
Thy followers of repentance, that their souls
May make a peaceful and a sweet retire
From off these fields where, wretches, their poor bodies
Must lie and fester.

KING HENRY
Who hath sent thee now?

MONTJOY
The constable of France.

KING HENRY
I pray thee, bear my former answer back.
Bid them achieve me and then sell my bones.
Good God, why should they mock poor fellows thus?
The man that once did sell the lion's skin
While the beast lived was killed with hunting him.
A many of our bodies shall no doubt
Find native graves, upon the which, I trust,
Shall witness live in brass of this day's work.
And those that leave their valiant bones in France,
Dying like men though buried in your dunghills,
They shall be famed; for there the sun shall greet them
And draw their honors reeking up to heaven,
Leaving their earthly parts to choke your clime,

KING HENRY

There! Now you've unwished five thousand men, which I prefer to your wishing for one more.—You know your places. God be with you all.

A trumpet sounds. MONTJOY *enters.*

MONTJOY

Once more I come to ask you, King Harry, if you're ready to negotiate your ransom before your certain defeat. For assuredly, you are so near the abyss that you're bound to be swallowed up. Moreover, out of mercy, the Constable urges you to remind your men to make their peace with God and repent, so that their souls may depart sweetly and peacefully from these fields where, poor wretches, their bodies will likely fall and fester.

KING HENRY

Who sent you this time?

MONTJOY

The Constable of France.

KING HENRY

Be good enough to take back the same answer I gave before. Tell them to capture me, then sell my bones. Good God! Why do they mock poor fellows this way? The man that once sold the skin of a lion while the beast still lived died hunting him. A good many of our bodies, I imagine, will end up in English soil. And on their graves, I trust, the story of this day's work will be written in brass. And those who leave their valiant bones in France, dying like men though buried in your dunghills—they'll be remembered, too. The sun will rise on them here and draw their glory up to heaven, leaving their mortal remains to choke your land: the smell of rotting flesh will breed a plague in France.

The smell whereof shall breed a plague in France.
Mark, then, abounding valor in our English,
That being dead, like to the bullet's crazing,
Break out into a second course of mischief,
Killing in relapse of mortality.
Let me speak proudly: tell the constable
We are but warriors for the working day;
Our gayness and our gilt are all besmirched
With rainy marching in the painful field.
There's not a piece of feather in our host—
Good argument, I hope, we will not fly—
And time hath worn us into slovenry.
But, by the Mass, our hearts are in the trim,
And my poor soldiers tell me, yet ere night
They'll be in fresher robes, or they will pluck
The gay new coats o'er the French soldiers' heads
And turn them out of service. If they do this,
As, if God please, they shall, my ransom then
Will soon be levied. Herald, save thou thy labor.
Come thou no more for ransom, gentle herald.
They shall have none, I swear, but these my joints,
Which, if they have, as I will leave 'em them,
Shall yield them little. Tell the constable.

MONTJOY

I shall, King Harry. And so fare thee well.
Thou never shalt hear herald anymore.

Exit

KING HENRY

I fear thou wilt once more come again for a ransom.

Enter YORK

Then will you notice the abundant valor of our Englishmen, who will embark on a second round of mischief like a ricocheting bullet, killing again as they fall to their deaths. Let me speak proudly: tell the Constable we're only workaday soldiers. Our finery and shining metal are all rusty from long, painful marches in the rain. There's not a strand of feather left in our whole army—a good sign, I hope, that we won't fly away like birds—and time on the field has made us slovenly. But, by God, our hearts are in good shape. And my poor soldiers tell me that before night they'll be in cleaner clothes. If not, they'll pull the bright new coats of the French over their heads and send them on their way. If they do this, as they will, God willing, my ransom will soon be raised. Herald, spare yourself. Don't come again to ask for my ransom, good messenger. I swear the only ransom will be these bones of mine. And if the French get them in the state in which I intend to leave them, they won't be worth much use to anyone. Tell the constable that.

MONTJOY

I shall, King Harry. And so farewell. You'll never hear from the herald again.

He exits.

KING HENRY

I'm afraid you'll come to me again for ransom.

YORK *enters.*

YORK

My lord, most humbly on my knee I beg
The leading of the vaward.

KING HENRY

Take it, brave York. Now, soldiers, march away,
And how Thou pleasest, God, dispose the day.

Exeunt

YORK

My lord, most humbly on bended knee I beg you to grant me the leading of the vanguard.

KING HENRY

Take it, brave York. Now, soldiers, advance. And you, God, bestow today's victory however it pleases You.

They all exit.

ACT 4, SCENE 4

Alarm, excursions. Enter **PISTOL**, **FRENCH SOLDIER**, *and* **BOY**

PISTOL
Yield, cur.

FRENCH SOLDIER
Je pense que vous êtes gentilhomme de bonne qualité.

PISTOL
Qualtitie calmie custure me. Art thou a gentleman? What is thy name? Discuss.

FRENCH SOLDIER
Ô Seigneur Dieu!

PISTOL
O Seigneur Dew should be a gentleman. Perpend my words, O Seigneur Dew, and mark: O Seigneur Dew, thou diest on point of fox, except, O Seigneur, thou do give to me egregious ransom.

FRENCH SOLDIER
Ô, prenez miséricorde! Ayez pitié de moi!

PISTOL
Moy shall not serve. I will have forty moys, or I will fetch thy rim out at thy throat in drops of crimson blood.

FRENCH SOLDIER
Est-il impossible d'échapper la force de ton bras?

ACT 4, SCENE 4

Sounds of battle. PISTOL, *a* FRENCH SOLDIER, *and the* BOY *enter.*

PISTOL

Surrender, dog!

FRENCH SOLDIER

(speaking in French) You seem like a gentleman of high rank.

PISTOL

Pistol is speaking nonsense as though it were a real foreign tongue.

Qualtitie calmie custure me! Are you a gentleman? What is your name? Expound.

FRENCH SOLDIER

(speaking in French) Oh, God above!

PISTOL

Pistol misunderstands the Frenchman to be saying his name is "O. Signieur Dew." Because "seigneur" means "lord," Pistol thinks his prisoner is a nobleman.

This man, one O. Signieur Dew, must be a gentleman. Consider my words, O. Signieur Dew, and take note: O. Signieur Dew, you'll be killed with my sword unless you pay me an absurd amount of money for your ransom.

FRENCH SOLDIER

(speaking in French) Oh, have mercy! Take pity on me!

PISTOL

(*mistaking* moi, *the French word for "me," as a unit of money*) One *moy* is not enough. I must have forty *moys*, or I will reach into your throat and pull out some *moys*, along with a lot of blood.

FRENCH SOLDIER

(speaking in French) Is it impossible to escape your mighty arm?

PISTOL
Brass, cur? Thou damned and luxurious mountain goat,
offer'st me brass?

FRENCH SOLDIER
Ô, pardonnez-moi!

PISTOL
Say'st thou me so? Is that a ton of moys?—Come hither,
boy. Ask me this slave in French what is his name.

BOY
Écoutez. Comment êtes-vous appelé?

FRENCH SOLDIER
Monsieur le Fer.

BOY
He says his name is Master Fer.

PISTOL
Master Fer. I'll fer him, and firk him, and ferret him.
Discuss the same in French unto him.

BOY
I do not know the French for "fer," and "ferret," and "firk."

PISTOL
Bid him prepare, for I will cut his throat.

FRENCH SOLDIER
(to the BOY*) Que dit-il, monsieur?*

BOY
Il me commande à vous dire que vous faites vous prêt, car ce soldat ici est disposé tout à cette heure de couper votre gorge.

PISTOL
Owy, cuppele gorge, permafoy, peasant, unless thou give
me crowns, brave crowns, or mangled shalt thou be by this
my sword.

PISTOL

(*mishearing* bras, *the French word for "arm," as "brass"*) Brass, you dog! You damned lazy mountain goat, do you offer me brass?

FRENCH SOLDIER

(*speaking in French*) Oh, spare me!

PISTOL

Really? Is that a lot of *moys*? Come over here, boy and ask this slave in French what his name is.

BOY

(*speaking in French*) Look, what's your name?

FRENCH SOLDIER

(*speaking in French*) Monsieur le Fer.

BOY

He says his name is Master Fer.

PISTOL

Firk = "beat"
Ferret = "tear"

Master Fer! I'll fer him, and firk him, and ferret him: expound as much to him in French.

BOY

I do not know the French for "fer," and "ferret," and "firk."

PISTOL

Tell him to prepare himself for death, for I'm going to cut his throat.

FRENCH SOLDIER

(*speaking in French, to the* BOY) What is he saying, sir?

BOY

(*speaking in French*) He told me to tell you to prepare to die, for this soldier here is of a mind to cut your throat without delay.

PISTOL

(*trying to speak French*) Yes, cut your throat, by God, you peasant, unless you give me gold coins, good gold coins. If not, you'll be mangled by this sword of mine.

FRENCH SOLDIER

Ô, je vous supplie, pour l'amour de Dieu, me pardoner. Je suis gentilhomme de bonne maison. Gardez ma vie, et je vous donnerai deux cents écus.

PISTOL

What are his words?

BOY

He prays you to save his life. He is a gentleman of a good house, and for his ransom he will give you two hundred crowns.

PISTOL

Tell him my fury shall abate, and I the crowns will take.

FRENCH SOLDIER

Petit monsieur, que dit-il?

BOY

Encore qu'il est contre son jurement de pardoner aucun prisonnier; néanmoins, pour les écus que vous lui avez promis, il est content à vous donner la liberté, le franchisement.

FRENCH SOLDIER

Sur mes genoux je vous donne mille remercîments, et je m'estime heureux que j'ai tombé entre les mains d'un chevalier, je pense, le plus brave, vaillant, et très distingué seigneur d'Angleterre.

PISTOL

Expound unto me, boy.

BOY

He gives you upon his knees a thousand thanks, and he esteems himself happy that he hath fall'n into the hands of one, as he thinks, the most brave, valorous, and thrice-worthy seigneur of England.

PISTOL

As I suck blood, I will some mercy show. Follow me.

FRENCH SOLDIER

(speaking in French) Oh, I beseech you, for the love of God, spare me! I am a gentleman of good family: spare me and I will give you two hundred *écus*.

PISTOL

What does he say?

BOY

He begs you to spare his life. He is a gentleman of a good family, and for his ransom, he will give you two hundred crowns.

PISTOL

Tell him my fury will abate, and I'll take the crowns.

FRENCH SOLDIER

(speaking in French) Young sir, what does he say?

BOY

(speaking in French) Once again, that it would be breaking his oath to pardon any prisoner. Nevertheless, for the crowns that you've promised him, he is willing to give you freedom, liberty.

FRENCH SOLDIER

(speaking in French) On my knees I thank you again and again. And I consider myself fortunate to have fallen into the hands of a knight—to my mind, the noblest, most valiant, and most distinguished gentleman of England.

PISTOL

Explain, boy.

BOY

He thanks you on his knees many times and considers himself fortunate to have fallen into the hands of one, as he thinks, who is the bravest, most valorous, and thrice-worthy gentleman of England.

PISTOL

As I get to leech him, I will show some mercy. Follow me.

BOY

Suivez-vous le grand capitaine.

Exeunt **PISTOL** *and* **FRENCH SOLDIER**

I did never know so full a voice issue from so empty a heart. But the saying is true: "The empty vessel makes the greatest sound." Bardolph and Nym had ten times more valor than this roaring devil i' th' old play, that everyone may pare his nails with a wooden dagger, and they are both hanged, and so would this be if he durst steal any thing adventurously. I must stay with the lackeys with the luggage of our camp. The French might have a good prey of us if he knew of it, for there is none to guard it but boys.

Exit

BOY

(speaking in French) Follow the mighty captain.

PISTOL *and the* FRENCH SOLDIER *exit.*

I never heard so loud a voice issue from such an empty heart. It's true what they say: "The empty vessel makes the greatest sound." Bardolph and Nym had ten times more courage than this roaring stage villain, whose nails any Joe could cut with a wooden dagger, but they are both hanged. So would this man if he had the nerve to steal anything bravely. I have to stay with the servants, who are with our camp's luggage. We're sitting ducks for the French, if they only knew it, for there is no one guarding it but boys.

He exits.

ACT 4, SCENE 5

Enter CONSTABLE, ORLÉANS, BOURBON, DAUPHIN, *and* RAMBURES

CONSTABLE
Ô diable!

ORLÉANS
Ô seigneur! Le jour est perdu, tout est perdu!

DAUPHIN
Mort de ma vie, all is confounded, all!
Reproach and everlasting shame
Sits mocking in our plumes.

A short alarum

Ô méchante Fortune!
Do not run away.

CONSTABLE
Why, all our ranks are broke.

DAUPHIN
O perdurable shame! Let's stab ourselves.
Be these the wretches that we played at dice for?

ORLÉANS
Is this the king we sent to for his ransom?

BOURBON
Shame, and eternal shame, nothing but shame!
Let us die. In once more! Back again!
And he that will not follow Bourbon now,
Let him go hence, and with his cap in hand
Like a base pander hold the chamber door,
Whilst by a slave, no gentler than my dog,
His fairest daughter is contaminate.

CONSTABLE
Disorder, that hath spoiled us, friend us now.
Let us on heaps go offer up our lives.

ACT 4, SCENE 5

The CONSTABLE *enters, with the Dukes of* ORLÉANS, BOURBON, *the* DAUPHIN, *and* RAMBURES.

CONSTABLE
O, hell!

ORLÉANS
O Lord, the day is lost! All is lost!

DAUPHIN
Dear God! All is lost, all! Regret and everlasting shame sit on our helmets, mocking us.

A brief blast of battle noises.

What stinking luck! Do not run away.

CONSTABLE
Our men have all broken ranks.

DAUPHIN
O, everlasting shame! Let's fall on our swords. Are these the wretches that we threw dice for?

ORLÉANS
Is this the king we offered to ransom?

BOURBON
Shame, eternal shame, and nothing but shame! Let us die honorably. Back into the fray once again! He who will not follow me now, let him depart and stand in the doorway like a pimp, cap in hand, while some slave, no nobler than my dog, violates his daughter.

CONSTABLE
Maybe we can benefit from the same chaos that has defeated us. Let's go offer up our lives *en masse*.

ORLÉANS
We are enough yet living in the field
To smother up the English in our throngs,
If any order might be thought upon.

BOURBON
The devil take order now! I'll to the throng.
Let life be short, else shame will be too long.

Exeunt

ORLÉANS

There are enough of us still alive in the field to overcome the English with our numbers if we could just restore some kind of order.

BOURBON

The hell with order! I'm going back into battle. Let life be short so that shame won't last too long.

They all exit.

ACT 4, SCENE 6

Alarum

Enter KING HENRY *and forces,* EXETER, *and others*

KING HENRY
Well have we done, thrice-valiant countrymen,
But all's not done. Yet keep the French the field.

EXETER
The duke of York commends him to your Majesty.

KING HENRY
Lives he, good uncle? Thrice within this hour
I saw him down, thrice up again and fighting.
From helmet to the spur, all blood he was.

EXETER
In which array, brave soldier, doth he lie,
Larding the plain, and by his bloody side,
Yoke-fellow to his honor-owing wounds,
The noble earl of Suffolk also lies.
Suffolk first died, and York, all haggled over,
Comes to him where in gore he lay insteeped
And takes him by the beard, kisses the gashes
That bloodily did yawn upon his face.
And cries aloud, "Tarry, my cousin Suffolk.
My soul shall thine keep company to heaven.
Tarry, sweet soul, for mine; then fly abreast,
As in this glorious and well-foughten field
We kept together in our chivalry."
Upon these words I came and cheered him up.
He smiled me in the face, raught me his hand,
And with a feeble grip, says "Dear my lord,
Commend my service to my sovereign."
So did he turn, and over Suffolk's neck

ACT 4, SCENE 6

Sounds of battle. KING HENRY *enters with soldiers,* EXETER, *and others.*

KING HENRY

We have done well, my valiant countrymen. But it's not over. The French are still fighting.

EXETER

The duke of York sends your Majesty his respects.

KING HENRY

Is he still alive, good uncle? Three times in an hour I saw him down, and three times up again and fighting. He was covered with blood from his helmet to his spurs.

EXETER

The valiant soldier is still dressed like that, lying on the ground, drenching the field with his blood. By his side lies the noble earl of Suffolk, York's comrade and equal in brave wounds. Suffolk died first, and York, cut to pieces, came to him where he lay in his blood and took him by the face, kissing his gashes. He cried out, "Wait for me, dear cousin. My soul will keep yours company on the way to heaven. Wait for mine, sweet soul. We'll fly there side by side, just as we stood together as brother-knights in this glorious and well-fought battle!" At this, I went to comfort him. He smiled at me close, gave me his hand, gripping me feebly, and said, "My dear lord, commend my service to my king." With that, he turned and threw his wounded arm around Suffolk's neck and kissed his

He threw his wounded arm and kissed his lips,
And so, espoused to death, with blood he sealed
A testament of noble-ending love.
The pretty and sweet manner of it forced
Those waters from me which I would have stopped,
But I had not so much of man in me,
And all my mother came into mine eyes
And gave me up to tears.

KING HENRY
I blame you not,
For, hearing this, I must perforce compound
With mistful eyes, or they will issue too.

Alarum

But hark, what new alarum is this same?
The French have reinforced their scattered men.
Then every soldier kill his prisoners.
Give the word through.

Exeunt

lips. And so, married to death, he sealed a testament of love that even ended in nobility. The fineness of the moment moved me to tears. I tried to hold them back, but wept like a mother.

KING HENRY

I don't blame you. Just listening, I have to school my misty eyes, or they will brim over.

Sounds of battle.

But listen! What new battle is this? The French have reinforced their scattered men. Then every soldier must kill his prisoners. Spread the word.

They all exit.

ACT 4, SCENE 7

Enter FLUELLEN *and* GOWER

FLUELLEN
Kill the poys and the luggage! 'Tis expressly against the law of arms. 'Tis as arrant a piece of knavery, mark you now, as can be offert, in your conscience now, is it not?

GOWER
'Tis certain there's not a boy left alive, and the cowardly rascals that ran from the battle ha' done this slaughter. Besides, they have burned and carried away all that was in the king's tent, wherefore the king, most worthily, hath caused every soldier to cut his prisoner's throat. Oh, 'tis a gallant king!

FLUELLEN
Ay, he was porn at Monmouth, Captain Gower. What call you the town's name where Alexander the Pig was born?

GOWER
Alexander the Great.

FLUELLEN
Why, I pray you, is not "pig" great? The pig, or the great, or the mighty, or the huge, or the magnanimous are all one reckonings, save the phrase is a little variations.

GOWER
I think Alexander the Great was born in Macedon. His father was called Philip of Macedon, as I take it.

FLUELLEN
I think it is in Macedon where Alexander is porn. I tell you, Captain, if you look in the maps of the 'orld, I warrant you shall find, in the comparisons between Macedon and Monmouth, that the situations, look you, is both alike.

ACT 4, SCENE 7

FLUELLEN *and* **GOWER** *enter.*

FLUELLEN

To kill the boys with the luggage! It's expressly against the rules of combat. It's as complete a work of villainy as any that could be thought up. Tell me, don't you think so?

GOWER

There's certainly not a boy left alive, and it was done by the cowardly rascals who were running from the battle. On top of this, they've either burned or carried away everything that was in the king's tent. So the king has quite rightly ordered that every prisoner's throat be cut. Oh, he's a gallant king!

FLUELLEN

Yes, he was born at Monmouth, Captain Gower. What is the name of the town where Alexander the Pig was born?

Fluellen pronounces p for b: he means "big."

GOWER

Alexander the Great.

FLUELLEN

And is "pig" not the same as "great," may I ask? The pig or the mighty or the huge or the magnanimous—they all mean the same thing, with some variation.

GOWER

I think Alexander the Great was born in Macedon. His father was Philip of Macedon, as I remember.

FLUELLEN

I think that Macedon is indeed where Alexander was born. I tell you, Captain, if you look at a map of the world, I'll bet you will find, comparing Macedon and Monmouth, that the situations, see, are very similar.

There is a river in Macedon, and there is also, moreover, a river at Monmouth. It is called Wye at Monmouth, but it is out of my prains what is the name of the other river. But 'tis all one; 'tis alike as my fingers is to my fingers, and there is salmons in both. If you mark Alexander's life well, Harry of Monmouth's life is come after it indifferent well, for there is figures in all things. Alexander, God knows and you know, in his rages and his furies and his wraths and his cholers and his moods and his displeasures and his indignations, and also being a little intoxicates in his prains, did, in his ales and his angers, look you, kill his best friend, Cleitus.

GOWER

Our king is not like him in that. He never killed any of his friends.

FLUELLEN

It is not well done, mark you now, to take the tales out of my mouth ere it is made and finished. I speak but in the figures and comparisons of it. As Alexander killed his friend Cleitus, being in his ales and his cups, so also Harry Monmouth, being in his right wits and his good judgments, turned away the fat knight with the great-belly doublet; he was full of jests, and gipes and knaveries, and mocks—I have forgot his name.

GOWER

Sir John Falstaff.

FLUELLEN

That is he. I'll tell you, there is good men porn at Monmouth.

GOWER

Here comes his Majesty.

There is a river in Macedon, and there is likewise a river in Monmouth. The river in Monmouth is called Wye, but the name of the other river has gone out of my head. Nevertheless, it's all one—the two rivers are as alike as my fingers are to my fingers, and there are salmon in both. If you look closely at Alexander's life, Harry of Monmouth's stands up fairly well by comparison—for there are analogies in everything. Alexander, God knows and you know, in his rages and his furies and his wraths and his angers and his moods and his displeasures and his indignations, and also being a little the worse for drink, killed his best friend Cleitus in a drunken rage, see.

GOWER

Our king is not like him in that respect: he never killed any of his friends.

FLUELLEN

It is not courteous, you know, to assume you know my meaning before I've finished talking. I'm speaking purely in analogies and comparisons. Just as Alexander killed his friend Cleitus when he was drinking, so Harry Monmouth, having come to his senses and acquired good judgment, turned away the fat knight in the oversized doublet: the man was full of jests and japes and pranks and mocks. I have forgotten his name.

GOWER

Sir John Falstaff.

FLUELLEN

That's the one. I tell you, there are good men born at Monmouth.

GOWER

Here comes his Majesty.

Alarum

Enter KING HENRY, WARWICK, GLOUCESTER, EXETER, *and others*

KING HENRY

I was not angry since I came to France
Until this instant. Take a trumpet, herald.
Ride thou unto the horsemen on yond hill.
If they will fight with us, bid them come down,
Or void the field. They do offend our sight.
If they'll do neither, we will come to them
And make them skirr away as swift as stones
Enforcèd from the old Assyrian slings.
Besides, we'll cut the throats of those we have,
And not a man of them that we shall take
Shall taste our mercy. Go and tell them so.

Enter MONTJOY

EXETER

Here comes the herald of the French, my liege.

GLOUCESTER

His eyes are humbler than they used to be.

KING HENRY

How now, what means this, herald? Know'st thou not
That I have fined these bones of mine for ransom?
Com'st thou again for ransom?

MONTJOY

No, great king.
I come to thee for charitable license,
That we may wander o'er this bloody field
To book our dead and then to bury them;
To sort our nobles from our common men,
For many of our princes—woe the while!—
Lie drowned and soaked in mercenary blood.
So do our vulgar drench their peasant limbs

Sounds of battle. **KING HENRY** *enters with* **WARWICK**, **GLOUCESTER**, **EXETER**, *and others.*

KING HENRY

I was not angry since I came to France until this instant. Take a trumpet, herald. Ride out to the horsemen on that hill. If they seek battle with us, have them come down or else clear the field. The sight of them is offensive. If they'll do neither, we'll come to them and make them fly like stones shot from powerful slings. We'll also cut the throats of any prisoners we have. Not a man of them that we shall take shall know our mercy. Go and tell them this.

MONTJOY *enters.*

EXETER

Here comes the herald of the French, my liege.

GLOUCESTER

He looks humbler than he used to.

KING HENRY

Well? What is the meaning of this, herald? Don't you know that I have offered these bones of mine for ransom? Are you coming again for ransom?

MONTJOY

No, great king. I come to ask you out of charity to let us wander over this bloody field to record the numbers of our dead and bury them, separating our nobles from the common men, for many of our princes—alas!—lie drowned and soaked in the blood of mercenary soldiers. Likewise, our common men lie drenched in the blood of princes, and their wounded steeds, ankle-deep in gore, struggle and, raging

In blood of princes, and the wounded steeds
Fret fetlock deep in gore, and with wild rage
Yerk out their armèd heels at their dead masters,
Killing them twice. Oh, give us leave, great king,
To view the field in safety and dispose
Of their dead bodies.

KING HENRY
I tell thee truly, herald,
I know not if the day be ours or no,
For yet a many of your horsemen peer
And gallop o'er the field.

MONTJOY
The day is yours.

KING HENRY
Praised be God, and not our strength, for it!
What is this castle called that stands hard by?

MONTJOY
They call it Agincourt.

KING HENRY
Then call we this the field of Agincourt,
Fought on the day of Crispin Crispianus.

FLUELLEN
Your grandfather of famous memory, an't please your Majesty, and your great-uncle Edward the Plack Prince of Wales, as I have read in the chronicles, fought a most prave pattle here in France.

KING HENRY
They did, Fluellen.

FLUELLEN
Your Majesty says very true. If your Majesties is remembered of it, the Welshmen did good service in a garden where leeks did grow, wearing leeks in their Monmouth caps, which, your Majesty know, to this hour is an honorable badge of the service. And I do believe your Majesty takes no scorn to wear the leek upon Saint Tavy's day.

wildly, stamp on their dead masters with their hooves, killing them a second time. Oh, give us permission, great king, to search the field in safety and dispose of our dead bodies.

KING HENRY

I'll be honest with you, herald: I don't even know who won the battle. I still see many of your horsemen galloping across the field.

MONTJOY

You won it.

KING HENRY

God, not our strength, be praised! What is the name of the castle that stands over there?

MONTJOY

Agincourt.

KING HENRY

Then we'll call this the Battle of Agincourt, fought on the day of Crispin Crispianus.

FLUELLEN

If I may say so, your Majesty, your famous grandfather and your great-uncle Edward, the Black Prince of Wales—or so I've read in the history books—fought a very brave battle here in France.

KING HENRY

They did, Fluellen.

FLUELLEN

Your Majesty is quite right. If your Majesties recall it, the Welsh fought very valiantly in a garden where there were leeks growing, wearing leeks in their Monmouth caps which, your Majesty knows, is to this day a badge of honorable military service. I do believe your Majesty takes no shame in wearing the leek on Saint Davy's Day.

KING HENRY

I wear it for a memorable honor,
For I am Welsh, you know, good countryman.

FLUELLEN

All the water in Wye cannot wash your Majesty's Welsh plood out of your pody, I can tell you that: God pless it and preserve it as long as it pleases his Grace and his Majesty too.

KING HENRY

Thanks, good my countryman.

FLUELLEN

By Jeshu, I am your Majesty's countryman, I care not who know it. I will confess it to all the 'orld. I need not to be ashamed of your Majesty, praised be God, so long as your Majesty is an honest man.

KING HENRY

God keep me so.—Our heralds go with him.
Bring me just notice of the numbers dead
On both our parts. *(points to* WILLIAMS*)*
Call yonder fellow hither.

Exeunt heralds with MONTJOY

EXETER

Soldier, you must come to the king.

KING HENRY

Soldier, why wear'st thou that glove in thy cap?

WILLIAMS

An't please your Majesty, 'tis the gage of one that I should fight withal, if he be alive.

KING HENRY

An Englishman?

WILLIAMS

An 't please your Majesty, a rascal that swaggered with me last night, who, if alive and ever dare to challenge this glove, I have sworn to take him a box o' th' ear, or if I can see my

KING HENRY

I wear it with pride, for I am Welsh you know, good countryman.

FLUELLEN

All the water in Wye cannot wash your Majesty's Welsh blood out of your body. I can tell you that. God bless it and preserve it, as long as it pleases his Grace, and his Majesty, too!

KING HENRY

Thanks, my good countryman.

FLUELLEN

By Jesus, I am your Majesty's countryman, and I don't care who knows it. I will confess it to all the world. I needn't be ashamed of your Majesty, God be praised, so long as your Majesty is an honest man.

KING HENRY

God keep me so.—Heralds, go with him. Bring me an exact report of the number of dead on both sides. *(pointing to* WILLIAMS*)* Tell that fellow over there to come here.

English messengers exit with MONTJOY.

EXETER

Soldier, you must come to the king.

KING HENRY

Soldier, why are you wearing that glove in your cap?

WILLIAMS

If it pleases your Majesty, it is the token of a man I must fight with, if he's still alive.

KING HENRY

An Englishman?

WILLIAMS

If I may say so, your Majesty, he is a rascal who quarreled with me last night, and who, if he lives and ever dares to challenge this glove, will get a box on the ear glove in his cap, which he swore, as he was a soldier, he would wear if alive, I will strike it out soundly.

KING HENRY
What think you, Captain Fluellen, is it fit this soldier keep his oath?

FLUELLEN
He is a craven and a villain else, an 't please your Majesty, in my conscience.

KING HENRY
It may be his enemy is a gentleman of great sort, quite from the answer of his degree.

FLUELLEN
Though he be as good a gentleman as the devil is, as Lucifer and Beelzebub himself, it is necessary, look your Grace, that he keep his vow and his oath. If he be perjured, see you now, his reputation is as arrant a villain and a Jack Sauce as ever his black shoe trod upon God's ground and His earth, in my conscience, la.

KING HENRY
Then keep thy vow, sirrah, when thou meet'st the fellow.

WILLIAMS
So I will, my liege, as I live.

KING HENRY
Who serv'st thou under?

WILLIAMS
Under Captain Gower, my liege.

FLUELLEN
Gower is a good captain, and is good knowledge and literatured in the wars.

KING HENRY
Call him hither to me, soldier.

WILLIAMS
I will, my liege.

Exit

from me. Or, if I see him wearing my glove in his cap, which he swore as a soldier he would wear if he lived, I will knock it off his head.

KING HENRY

What do you say, Captain Fluellen? Should this soldier keep his oath?

FLUELLEN

If I may say so, your Majesty, as I see it he would be a coward and a villain not to.

KING HENRY

It may be that his antagonist is a gentleman of very high degree, quite outside of his own sphere.

FLUELLEN

Even if he were as important a man as the devil—as Lucifer or Beelzebub himself—he's required, see, your Grace, to keep his vow. If he backs down, he'll become as notorious a villain and as saucy a Jack as ever walked on God's earth, in my opinion.

KING HENRY

Then keep your vow, fellow, when you meet the man.

WILLIAMS

So I will, my liege. I swear on my life.

KING HENRY

Whom do you serve under?

WILLIAMS

Under Captain Gower, my liege.

FLUELLEN

Gower is a good captain, and is well versed and well read in the wars.

KING HENRY

Have him come to me here, soldier.

WILLIAMS

I will, my liege.

He exits.

KING HENRY
Here, Fluellen, wear thou this favor for me and stick it in thy cap. *(gives* WILLIAMS*'s glove to* FLUELLEN*)* When Alençon and myself were down together, I plucked this glove from his helm. If any man challenge this, he is a friend to Alençon and an enemy to our person. If thou encounter any such, apprehend him, an thou dost me love.

FLUELLEN
Your Grace does me as great honors as can be desired in the hearts of his subjects. I would fain see the man that has but two legs that shall find himself aggrieved at this glove, that is all; but I would fain see it once, an please God of his Grace that I might see.

KING HENRY
Know'st thou Gower?

FLUELLEN
He is my dear friend, an please you.

KING HENRY
Pray thee, go seek him, and bring him to my tent.

FLUELLEN
I will fetch him.

Exit

KING HENRY
My Lord of Warwick and my brother Gloucester,
Follow Fluellen closely at the heels.
The glove which I have given him for a favor
May haply purchase him a box o' th' ear.
It is the soldier's. I by bargain should
Wear it myself. Follow, good cousin Warwick.

KING HENRY

Here, Fluellen, stick this in your cap. *(gives* **WILLIAMS***'s glove to* **FLUELLEN***)* When Alençon and I went down together, I plucked this glove from his helmet. If any man challenges it, he is a friend to Alençon and an enemy to me. If you encounter such a man, arrest him and prove your loyalty to me.

FLUELLEN

Your Grace does me as great an honor as could be wished by any of his subjects. I'd like to see the man with two legs who takes offense at this glove, that's all! Just once I'd like to see it, if it please God to grant me that.

KING HENRY

Do you know Captain Gower?

FLUELLEN

He is my dear friend, your Majesty.

KING HENRY

Go find him, please, and bring him to my tent.

FLUELLEN

I'll fetch him.

He exits.

KING HENRY

My Lord of Warwick and my brother Gloucester, follow Fluellen at a close distance. The glove which I have given him to wear may possibly win him a box on the ear. It belongs to the soldier I was just talking to. According to an agreement, I should wear it myself. Follow Fluellen, cousin Warwick, and if the soldier

If that the soldier strike him, as I judge
By his blunt bearing he will keep his word,
Some sudden mischief may arise of it,
For I do know Fluellen valiant
And, touched with choler, hot as gunpowder,
And quickly will return an injury.
Follow, and see there be no harm between them.
—Go you with me, uncle of Exeter.

Exeunt

strikes him—and I would think from his forthright manner that he'll keep his word—some mischief may arise as a result. I know Fluellen to be very conscious of his honor and quick to anger, hot as gunpowder and likely to return any injury promptly. Follow and see to it that nothing serious happens between them. You come with me, uncle of Exeter.

They all exit.

ACT 4, SCENE 8

Enter GOWER *and* WILLIAMS

WILLIAMS
I warrant it is to knight you, Captain.

Enter FLUELLEN

FLUELLEN
God's will and His pleasure, Captain, I beseech you now, come apace to the king. There is more good toward you peradventure than is in your knowledge to dream of.

WILLIAMS
Sir, know you this glove?

FLUELLEN
Know the glove! I know the glove is a glove.

WILLIAMS
I know this, and thus I challenge it. *(strikes him)*

FLUELLEN
'Sblood, an arrant traitor as any 's in the universal world, or in France, or in England!

GOWER
How now, sir? You villain!

WILLIAMS
Do you think I'll be forsworn?

FLUELLEN
Stand away, Captain Gower. I will give treason his payment into plows, I warrant you.

WILLIAMS
I am no traitor.

FLUELLEN
That's a lie in thy throat.—I charge you in his Majesty's name, apprehend him. He's a friend of the Duke Alençon's.

ACT 4, SCENE 8

GOWER *and* WILLIAMS *enter.*

WILLIAMS

I'm sure it is to knight you, Captain.

FLUELLEN *enters, wearing* WILLIAMS*'s glove.*

FLUELLEN

As it is God's will and pleasure, Captain, I entreat you to come quickly to the king. There is more good fortune in store for you than you could ever imagine.

WILLIAMS

Sir, do you recognize this glove?

FLUELLEN

Know the glove! I know the glove is a glove.

WILLIAMS

Well, I recognize this one *(indicates the glove* FLUELLEN *wears in his cap)*, and I hereby challenge you. *(strikes him)*

FLUELLEN

Good God! As absolute a traitor as any in the whole entire world—or even France or England!

GOWER

What is this, you villain!

WILLIAMS

Do you think I'd break my oath?

FLUELLEN

Stand aside, Captain Gower. I'll reward treason with blows, I promise you.

WILLIAMS

I'm not a traitor.

FLUELLEN

An infamous lie! I accuse you in the name of the king. Arrest him: he's a friend of the duke of Alençon's.

Enter WARWICK *and* GLOUCESTER

WARWICK
How now, how now, what's the matter?

FLUELLEN
My Lord of Warwick, here is, praised be God for it, a most contagious treason come to light, look you, as you shall desire in a summer's day.

Enter KING HENRY *and* EXETER

Here is his Majesty.

KING HENRY
How now, what's the matter?

FLUELLEN
My liege, here is a villain and a traitor, that, look your Grace, has struck the glove which your Majesty is take out of the helmet of Alençon.

WILLIAMS
My liege, this was my glove; here is the fellow of it. And he that I gave it to in change promised to wear it in his cap. I promised to strike him if he did. I met this man with my glove in his cap, and I have been as good as my word.

FLUELLEN
Your Majesty, hear now, saving your Majesty's manhood, what an arrant, rascally, beggarly, lousy knave it is. I hope your Majesty is pear me testimony and witness, and will avouchment that this is the glove of Alençon that your Majesty is give me, in your conscience now.

KING HENRY
Give me thy glove, soldier. Look, here is the fellow of it.
'Twas I indeed thou promised'st to strike,
And thou hast given me most bitter terms.

WARWICK *and* GLOUCESTER *enter.*

WARWICK
Now, now! What's all this? What's going on?

FLUELLEN
My Lord of Warwick, a most corrupt treason—God be praised for it!—has been discovered, as plain as any you'd hope to see on a summer's day. Here is his Majesty.

KING HENRY *and* EXETER *enter.*

KING HENRY
Well, now! What's the matter?

FLUELLEN
My liege, this man is a villain and a traitor, who—see, your Grace—has struck the glove which your Majesty took from Alençon's helmet.

WILLIAMS
My liege, this was my glove. Here is its mate, and the man I gave it to promised to wear it in his cap, and I promised to strike him if he did. I met this man with my glove in his cap, and I have been as good as my word.

FLUELLEN
Your Majesty, see here—if it won't offend your Grace—what a complete, rascally, beggarly, lousy rat this is. I hope your Majesty will, in all good conscience, bear me out and vouch for the fact that this is the glove of Alençon and that your Majesty gave it to me.

KING HENRY
Give me your glove, soldier: look, here is its mate. It was I, in fact, whom you promised to strike. And you spoke of me in the harshest terms.

FLUELLEN
An please your Majesty, let his neck answer for it, if there is any martial law in the world.

KING HENRY
How canst thou make me satisfaction?

WILLIAMS
All offenses, my lord, come from the heart. Never came any from mine that might offend your Majesty.

KING HENRY
It was ourself thou didst abuse.

WILLIAMS
Your Majesty came not like yourself. You appeared to me but as a common man. Witness the night, your garments, your lowliness. And what your Highness suffered under that shape, I beseech you take it for your own fault and not mine, for, had you been as I took you for, I made no offense. Therefore, I beseech your Highness pardon me.

KING HENRY
Here, uncle Exeter, fill this glove with crowns
And give it to this fellow.—Keep it, fellow,
And wear it for an honor in thy cap
Till I do challenge it.—Give him the crowns.
—And, captain, you must needs be friends with him.

FLUELLEN
By this day and this light, the fellow has mettle enough in his belly.—Hold, there is twelve pence for you, and I pray you to serve God and keep you out of prawls and prabbles and quarrels and dissensions, and I warrant you it is the better for you.

WILLIAMS
I will none of your money.

FLUELLEN

If it pleases your Majesty, let his neck pay the price, if there is any martial law in the world.

KING HENRY

How can you square things with me?

WILLIAMS

All offenses come from the heart, my lord, and nothing intended to offend your Majesty ever came from mine.

KING HENRY

You abused me to my face.

WILLIAMS

Your Majesty didn't present yourself as the king. You represented yourself as just a common man. Consider the time of night, what you were wearing, and how ordinary you looked. Anything your Highness suffered in that disguise, I beg you to see it as your own fault and not mine, because if you'd been what I took you for, there would have been no offense. Therefore, I beg your Highness, pardon me.

KING HENRY

Here, uncle Exeter, fill this glove with gold coins and give it to this fellow. Keep it, my friend, and wear it as a badge of honor in your cap until I challenge it.—Give him the money.—And you, Captain, must make it up with him.

FLUELLEN

By this day and this light, the fellow is certainly brave. Here, twelve pence for you. I urge you to serve God and stay out of brawls and dust-ups and quarrels and disputes. I promise it will be better for you if you do.

WILLIAMS

I'll have none of your money.

FLUELLEN
It is with a good will. I can tell you it will serve you to mend your shoes. Come, wherefore should you be so pashful? Your shoes is not so good. 'Tis a good silling, I warrant you, or I will change it.

Enter an English HERALD

KING HENRY
Now, herald, are the dead numbered?

HERALD
Here is the number of the slaughtered French.

KING HENRY
What prisoners of good sort are taken, uncle?

EXETER
Charles, duke of Orléans, nephew to the king;
John, duke of Bourbon, and Lord Bouciqualt.
Of other lords and barons, knights and squires,
Full fifteen hundred, besides common men.

KING HENRY
This note doth tell me of ten thousand French
That in the field lie slain. Of princes in this number
And nobles bearing banners, there lie dead
One hundred twenty-six. Added to these,
Of knights, esquires, and gallant gentlemen,
Eight thousand and four hundred, of the which,
Five hundred were but yesterday dubbed knights.
So that in these ten thousand they have lost,
There are but sixteen hundred mercenaries.
The rest are princes, barons, lords, knights, squires,
And gentlemen of blood and quality.
The names of those their nobles that lie dead:
Charles Delabreth, high constable of France;
Jaques of Chatillon, admiral of France;
The Master of the Crossbows, Lord Rambures;

FLUELLEN

It's meant in good will. I tell you, you can use it to get your shoes fixed. Come, why be so hesitant? Your shoes are in pretty bad shape. It's a good shilling, I promise you. If not, I'll get another one for you.

An English HERALD *enters.*

KING HENRY

Now, herald, have the dead been counted?

HERALD

Here is the count of the slaughtered French.

KING HENRY

What prisoners of rank have been taken, uncle?

EXETER

Charles duke of Orléans, nephew to the king; John duke of Bourbon, and Lord Bouciqualt: of other lords and barons, knights and squires, a full fifteen hundred, besides common men.

KING HENRY

This paper tells me of ten thousand Frenchmen who lie dead on the battlefield. Among them are one hundred twenty-six princes and standard-bearing nobles. Add to these eight thousand four hundred knights, squires, and brave gentlemen, five hundred of whom were given the title of knight only yesterday. Among the ten thousand the French have lost only sixteen hundred are mercenaries. The rest of the dead are princes, barons, lords, knights, squires, and gentlemen of birth and rank. The names of those of their nobles that lie dead: Charles Delabreth, high constable of France; Jaques of Chatillon, admiral of France; the master of the crossbows, Lord Rambures; Great

Great Master of France, the brave Sir Guichard Dauphin;
John, duke of Alençon; Anthony, duke of Brabant,
The brother of the duke of Burgundy,
And Edward, duke of Bar. Of lusty earls:
Grandpré and Roussi, Faulconbridge and Foix,
Beaumont and Marle, Vaudemont and Lestrale.
Here was a royal fellowship of death.
Where is the number of our English dead?

HERALD *shows him another paper*

Edward the duke of York, the earl of Suffolk,
Sir Richard Ketly, Davy Gam, esquire;
None else of name, and of all other men
But five and twenty. O God, thy arm was here,
And not to us but to thy arm alone
Ascribe we all! When, without stratagem,
But in plain shock and even play of battle,
Was ever known so great and little loss
On one part and on th' other? Take it, God,
For it is none but thine.

EXETER

'Tis wonderful.

KING HENRY

Come, go we in procession to the village,
And be it death proclaimèd through our host
To boast of this or take that praise from God
Which is His only.

FLUELLEN

Is it not lawful, an please your Majesty, to tell how many is killed?

KING HENRY

Yes, Captain, but with this acknowledgement:
That God fought for us.

FLUELLEN

Yes, my conscience, He did us great good.

Master of France, the brave Sir Guichard Dolphin, John duke of Alençon, Anthony duke of Brabant, the brother of the duke of Burgundy, and Edward duke of Bar. Of brave earls, Grandpré and Roussi, Fauconberg and Foix, Beaumont and Marle, Vaudemont and Lestrale. Here was a royal fellowship of death! Where is the number of our English dead?

The HERALD *shows him another paper.*

Edward the duke of York, the earl of Suffolk, Sir Richard Ketly, Davy Gam, esquire. No one else of name, and only twenty-five other men. Oh, God, your power was with us. What happened here is your doing alone, not ours. When was there ever before so great a loss on one side and so little on the other, in the ordinary and equal clash of battle? Take credit, God, for it is no one's doing but yours.

EXETER

It's unbelievable.

KING HENRY

Come, let's make a solemn procession to the village. And let it be proclaimed throughout our army that it shall be a hanging offense for anyone to boast of this or take from God the credit that belongs to Him alone.

FLUELLEN

If it pleases your Majesty, isn't it permissible to mention the number of casualties?

KING HENRY

Yes, Captain, but with this acknowledgement—that God fought for us.

FLUELLEN

Yes, I truly think He did great good.

KING HENRY

Do we all holy rites.
Let there be sung *Non nobis* and *Te Deum,*
The dead with charity enclosed in clay,
And then to Calais, and to England then,
Where ne'er from France arrived more happy men.

Exeunt

KING HENRY

We'll perform all the holy rites. Let *Non nobis* and *Te Deum* be sung, and let the dead be buried properly. Then on to Calais and from there to England. There have never been more fortunate men than we to return from France.

They all exit.

ACT FIVE

PROLOGUE

Enter CHORUS

CHORUS

Vouchsafe to those that have not read the story
That I may prompt them; and of such as have,
I humbly pray them to admit th' excuse
Of time, of numbers, and due course of things,
Which cannot in their huge and proper life
Be here presented. Now we bear the king
Toward Calais. Grant him there. There seen,
Heave him away upon your wingèd thoughts
Athwart the sea. Behold, the English beach
Pales in the flood with men, with wives and boys,
Whose shouts and claps outvoice the deep-mouthed sea,
Which like a mighty whiffler 'fore the king
Seems to prepare his way. So let him land,
And solemnly see him set on to London.
So swift a pace hath thought that even now
You may imagine him upon Blackheath,
Where that his lords desire him to have borne
His bruisèd helmet and his bended sword
Before him through the city. He forbids it,
Being free from vainness and self-glorious pride,
Giving full trophy, signal, and ostent
Quite from himself, to God. But now behold,
In the quick forge and workinghouse of thought,
How London doth pour out her citizens.
The Mayor and all his brethren in best sort,
Like to the senators of th' antique Rome,
With the plebeians swarming at their heels,
Go forth and fetch their conquering Caesar in—
As, by a lower but loving likelihood,

ACT FIVE

PROLOGUE

The CHORUS *enters.*

CHORUS

Allow me to fill in the gaps for those of you who have not read this story. As for those who have, I beg you to excuse the gaps in time, and the many people and things that cannot be represented here in all their magnitude and proper form. Let's bring the king now to Calais. Imagine him there and, having seen him there, haul him back across the sea on the wings of your imagination. There's the coast of England: see how the sea seems to be fenced in by the men and wives and boys who line the shore, their shouts and wild applause drowning out the deep roar of the surf. As the king's ship draws near, the very ocean is like a man running before the king, preparing his way. Let's have him land and solemnly proceed to London. Thoughts work so quickly that even now you can imagine him on Blackheath, where his lords suggest that he should carry his battle-scarred sword and helmet on a procession through the city. He refuses, as he is free of vanity and self-serving pride and ascribes all the glory and responsibility for victory to God. Now in the factory of thought, create the image of all London pouring forth into the streets. Picture the mayor and all his brother citizens dressed in their best as they go forth like senators of ancient Rome to welcome home their conquering Caesar. Imagine if our own queen's general returned from Ireland, having stamped out the rebellion there, as we hope he does very soon, how many people would leave the city to come welcome him. Even more people than that wel-

Were now the general of our gracious empress,
As in good time he may, from Ireland coming,
Bringing rebellion broachèd on his sword,
How many would the peaceful city quit
To welcome him! Much more, and much more cause,
Did they this Harry. Now in London place him
(As yet the lamentation of the French
Invites the king of England's stay at home;
The emperor's coming in behalf of France
To order peace between them) and omit
All the occurrences, whatever chanced,
Till Harry's back return again to France.
There must we bring him, and myself have played
The interim, by remembering you 'tis past.
Then brook abridgment, and your eyes advance
After your thoughts, straight back again to France.

Exit

comed Harry home, and they had even more reason. Let's put him now in London, since France's period of mourning requires the king of England to stay home. Imagine a visit of the Holy Roman Emperor, working on France's behalf. He wants to bring about a peace between the two countries. Skip over all the particularities between then and Harry's return to France. There we must place him, and I myself have covered the interim period by reminding you that it has taken place. So, keeping this omission in mind, immediately return to France, your eyes following the path of your thoughts.

The CHORUS *exits.*

ACT 5, SCENE 1

Enter FLUELLEN *and* GOWER

GOWER
Nay, that's right. But why wear you your leek today? Saint Davy's day is past.

FLUELLEN
There is occasions and causes why and wherefore in all things. I will tell you as my friend, Captain Gower. The rascally, scald, beggarly, lousy, pragging knave, Pistol, which you and yourself and all the world know to be no petter than a fellow, look you now, of no merits, he is come to me and prings me pread and salt yesterday, look you, and bid me eat my leek. It was in place where I could not breed no contention with him, but I will be so bold as to wear it in my cap till I see him once again, and then I will tell him a little piece of my desires.

Enter PISTOL

GOWER
Why, here he comes, swelling like a turkey-cock.

FLUELLEN
'Tis no matter for his swellings, nor his turkey-cocks.—God pless you, Aunchient Pistol, you scurvy, lousy knave, God pless you.

PISTOL
Ha, art thou bedlam? Dost thou thirst, base Trojan, to have me fold up Parca's fatal web? Hence. I am qualmish at the smell of leek.

FLUELLEN
I peseech you heartily, scurvy, lousy knave, at my desires, and my requests, and my petitions, to eat, look you, this leek. Because, look you, you do not love it, nor your affections and your appetites and your digestions does not agree with it, I would desire you to eat it.

ACT 5, SCENE 1

FLUELLEN *and* GOWER *enter.*

GOWER

Yes, that's true, but why are you wearing your leek today? Saint Davy's Day has passed.

FLUELLEN

There are reasons and causes why and how in everything. I'll tell you as my friend, Captain Gower: that rascally, mean, beggarly, lousy, bragging Pistol, whom you and yourself and all the world know to be no better than a peasant—see—with no good qualities at all: he came to me yesterday and brought me bread and salt and told me to eat my leek. We were somewhere where I couldn't pick a fight with him, but I've decided to wear it in my cap until I see him again, whereupon I'll give him a little piece of my mind.

PISTOL *enters.*

GOWER

And here he comes, puffing himself up like a turkey.

FLUELLEN

Never mind his puffings and his turkeys. God bless you, Ensign Pistol! You lousy, rotten, villain, God bless you!

PISTOL

Are you mad? Do you want me to cut your life short, you deceiving lowlife? Away! The smell of leek turns my stomach.

FLUELLEN

I wonder if you'd be so good, you lousy, rotten villain, to grant my wish and my request and gratify me, see, by eating this leek. I'd like you to, see, because you don't like it, and because it isn't to your taste, and because it doesn't agree with you.

PISTOL
Not for Cadwallader and all his goats.

FLUELLEN
There is one goat for you. (strikes him) Will you be so good, scald knave, as eat it?

PISTOL
Base Trojan, thou shalt die.

FLUELLEN
You say very true, scald knave, when God's will is. I will desire you to live in the meantime and eat your victuals. Come, there is sauce for it. (strikes him) You called me yesterday "mountain squire," but I will make you today a squire of low degree. I pray you, fall to. If you can mock a leek, you can eat a leek.

GOWER
Enough, Captain. You have astonished him.

FLUELLEN
I say I will make him eat some part of my leek, or I will peat his pate four days.—Bite, I pray you. It is good for your green wound and your ploody coxcomb.

PISTOL
Must I bite?

FLUELLEN
Yes, certainly, and out of doubt and out of question, too, and ambiguities.

PISTOL
By this leek, I will most horribly revenge. I eat and eat, I swear—

FLUELLEN
Eat, I pray you. Will you have some more sauce to your leek? There is not enough leek to swear by.

PISTOL
Quiet thy cudgel. Thou dost see I eat.

PISTOL

Not for Cadwallader and all his goats.

FLUELLEN

Here's a goat for you. (*strikes him with a club*) Will you be good enough to eat it, mangy rascal?

PISTOL

Dissolute lowlife, you shall die.

FLUELLEN

That's very true, mangy rascal, when it pleases God. Meanwhile, I'd be gratified if you'd live and eat your food. Come, here's some sauce to go with it. (*strikes him with his club*) Yesterday you called me "mountain squire." Today I'll make you squire of the low ground. Go on, eat up. If you can mock a leek, you can eat a leek.

GOWER

Enough, Captain. You've stunned him.

FLUELLEN

I tell you, I'll either make him eat some part of this leek or give him a four-day head-bashing.—Go on, bite. It's good for your fresh wound and your bloody noggin.

PISTOL

Must I bite?

FLUELLEN

Yes, absolutely, no question or ambiguity about it.

PISTOL

By this leek, I swear I'll make you pay for this. (FLUELLEN *threatens to strike him*) Okay, okay, I'm eating it—

FLUELLEN

Please do. Would you like some more sauce to go with it? There isn't enough leek left for you to swear on.

PISTOL

Lay off, already! Can't you see I'm eating?

FLUELLEN

Much good do you, scald knave, heartily. Nay, pray you throw none away. The skin is good for your broken coxcomb. When you take occasions to see leeks hereafter, I pray you, mock at 'em, that is all.

PISTOL

Good.

FLUELLEN

Ay, leeks is good. Hold you, there is a groat to heal your pate.

PISTOL

Me, a groat?

FLUELLEN

Yes, verily, and in truth you shall take it, or I have another leek in my pocket, which you shall eat.

PISTOL

I take thy groat in earnest of revenge.

FLUELLEN

If I owe you anything, I will pay you in cudgels. You shall be a woodmonger and buy nothing of me but cudgels. God be wi' you and keep you and heal your pate.

Exit

PISTOL

All hell shall stir for this.

GOWER

Go, go. You are a counterfeit cowardly knave. Will you mock at an ancient tradition begun upon an honorable respect and worn as a memorable trophy of predeceased valor, and dare not avouch in your deeds any of your words? I have seen you gleeking and galling at this gentleman twice or thrice. You thought because he could not speak English in the native garb, he could not therefore handle an English cudgel. You find it otherwise, and henceforth let a Welsh correction teach you a good English condition. Fare you well.

FLUELLEN

I sincerely hope it does you good, mangy rascal. No, don't throw any of it away. The skin is good for your cracked head. When you see leeks in the future, I hope you keep mocking them. That's all.

PISTOL

Good.

FLUELLEN

Yes, leeks are good. Wait, here's a penny to heal your head.

PISTOL

Me, a penny?

FLUELLEN

Yes, and you'll take it. If not, I have another leek in my pocket that you can eat.

PISTOL

I'll take this penny as a token that you'll pay for this.

FLUELLEN

If I owe you anything, I'll pay you in clubbings. You'll become a wood salesman and buy nothing but clubs from me. God be with you and keep you, and may he heal your head.

He exits.

PISTOL

There'll be hell to pay for this.

GOWER

Go on, get out of here. You're a lying, cowardly wretch. You mock an ancient tradition, born of reverence and worn in honor of brave men who have died, and then have the gall not to stand by your words. I've seen you bait and mock this man more than once. You thought because he didn't speak English like a native he couldn't handle an English club. You've learned otherwise. Let this be a Welsh lesson to you to behave with English manners in the future. Farewell.

Exit

PISTOL

Doth Fortune play the huswife with me now?
News have I that my Nell is dead i' th' spital
Of a malady of France,
And there my rendezvous is quite cut off.
Old I do wax, and from my weary limbs
Honor is cudgeled. Well, bawd I'll turn,
And something lean to cutpurse of quick hand.
To England will I steal, and there I'll steal.
And patches will I get unto these cudgeled scars,
And swear I got them in the Gallia wars.

Exit

He exits.

PISTOL

Has Fortune turned on me, like the whore she is? I've had news that my Nell died of the pox in a hospice. There went my last refuge. I grow old, and all dignity has been thrashed out of me. Well, I'll turn pimp and do some occasional pickpocketing. I'll steal away to England, and I'll steal some more when I get there. I'll bandage up these wounds and swear I got them in the French wars.

He exits.

ACT 5, SCENE 2

Enter at one door KING HENRY, EXETER, BEDFORD, GLOUCESTER, WARWICK, WESTMORELAND, *and other lords; at another, the* FRENCH KING, QUEEN ISABEL, *the princess* KATHERINE, ALICE *and other ladies; the Duke of* BURGUNDY, *and his train*

KING HENRY
Unto our brother France and to our sister,
Health and fair time of day.—Joy and good wishes
To our most fair and princely cousin Katherine.—
And, as a branch and member of this royalty,
By whom this great assembly is contrived,
We do salute you, Duke of Burgundy.—
And princes French, and peers, health to you all. Peace to this meeting wherefore we are met.

KING OF FRANCE
Right joyous are we to behold your face,
Most worthy brother England. Fairly met.
—So are you, princes English, every one.

QUEEN ISABEL
So happy be the issue, brother England,
Of this good day and of this gracious meeting,
As we are now glad to behold your eyes—
Your eyes which hitherto have borne in them
Against the French that met them in their bent
The fatal balls of murdering basilisks.
The venom of such looks, we fairly hope,
Have lost their quality, and that this day
Shall change all griefs and quarrels into love.

KING HENRY
To cry "Amen" to that, thus we appear.

QUEEN ISABEL
You English princes all, I do salute you.

ACT 5, SCENE 2

Through one door KING HENRY, EXETER, BEDFORD, GLOUCESTER, WARWICK, WESTMORELAND, *and other lords enter. Through another door, the* FRENCH KING, QUEEN ISABEL, *the princess* KATHERINE, ALICE, *and other ladies enter with the* DUKE OF BURGUNDY *and his train.*

KING HENRY
Peace to this occasion that's brought us all together. Health and good day to our brother the king of France and to our sister the queen. Joy and good wishes to our lovely royal cousin, Katherine. And you, Duke of Burgundy, who brought this great assembly together, we salute you as descendent and member of this royal family. And a health to all you lords and princes of France.

KING OF FRANCE
We rejoice to see you, most worthy brother of England. You are welcome here, as are all of you English princes.

QUEEN ISABEL
Brother of England, may this meeting prove as fruitful as it is joyous. We are glad to look upon your face—a face whose eyes have until now carried in them a glance as deadly, for any Frenchman they alighted on, as the poisonous eyes of those mythical lizards, the basilisks. We hope your poison has worn off and this day shall transform all grievances and quarrels into friendship.

KING HENRY
We're here to say "amen" to that.

QUEEN ISABEL
All you English princes, I salute you.

BURGUNDY

My duty to you both, on equal love,
Great kings of France and England. That I have labored
With all my wits, my pains, and strong endeavors,
To bring your most imperial Majesties
Unto this bar and royal interview,
Your mightiness on both parts best can witness.
Since, then, my office hath so far prevailed
That face to face and royal eye to eye
You have congreeted. Let it not disgrace me
If I demand before this royal view
What rub or what impediment there is
Why that the naked, poor, and mangled peace,
Dear nurse of arts, plenties, and joyful births,
Should not in this best garden of the world,
Our fertile France, put up her lovely visage?
Alas, she hath from France too long been chased,
And all her husbandry doth lie on heaps,
Corrupting in its own fertility.
Her vine, the merry cheerer of the heart,
Unprunèd, dies. Her hedges, even-pleached,
Like prisoners wildly overgrown with hair,
Put forth disordered twigs. Her fallow leas
The darnel, hemlock, and rank fumitory
Doth root upon, while that the coulter rusts
That should deracinate such savagery.
The even mead, that erst brought sweetly forth
The freckled cowslip, burnet, and green clover,
Wanting the scythe, withal uncorrected, rank,
Conceives by idleness, and nothing teems
But hateful docks, rough thistles, kecksies, burrs,
Losing both beauty and utility.
And as our vineyards, fallows, meads, and hedges,
Defective in their natures, grow to wildness,
Even so our houses and ourselves and children
Have lost, or do not learn for want of time,

BURGUNDY

Great kings of France and England, I owe you both equal service and loyalty. Your Highnesses can both attest to the fact that I've strived mightily, with all my wits and energy, to bring about this royal meeting between you two imperial Majesties. Since I have succeeded to the point of bringing you face to face and eye to eye, don't take it ill if I formally demand to know, before this royal congregation, what obstacle or impediment prevents the poor fragile, mangled peace, the mother of arts and joyous births, from showing her lovely face in this most fertile garden of the world, our fair France? Alas, she has been too long exiled from France, whose crops all lie in heaps, rotting with ripeness. Her grapes, which make the wine that cheers our hearts, die unpruned on the vines. Her once-trimmed hedges, like prisoners with wild, untended hair, put forth unruly twigs. Her fallow fields are overgrown with weeds, while the blade that should uproot such wilderness lies rusting. The level meadow, where the freckled cowslip, burnet, and green clover once grew, has become useless: unmowed, it grows to seed, so that nothing springs up but weeds, rough thistles, barren plants, and burs.
And just as our vineyards, fallow fields, meadows, and hedges, which grow improperly if left to themselves, run riot, so our families and ourselves and our

The sciences that should become our country,
But grow like savages, as soldiers will
That nothing do but meditate on blood,
To swearing and stern looks, diffused attire,
And everything that seems unnatural.
Which to reduce into our former favor
You are assembled, and my speech entreats
That I may know the let why gentle peace
Should not expel these inconveniences
And bless us with her former qualities.

KING HENRY

If, Duke of Burgundy, you would the peace,
Whose want gives growth to th' imperfections
Which you have cited, you must buy that peace
With full accord to all our just demands,
Whose tenors and particular effects
You have, enscheduled briefly, in your hands.

BURGUNDY

The king hath heard them, to the which as yet
There is no answer made.

KING HENRY

Well then, the peace which you before so urged
Lies in his answer.

KING OF FRANCE

I have but with a cursitory eye
O'erglanced the articles. Pleaseth your Grace
To appoint some of your council presently
To sit with us once more with better heed
To resurvey them, we will suddenly
Pass our accept and peremptory answer.

KING HENRY

Brother, we shall.—Go, uncle Exeter,
And brother Clarence, and you, brother Gloucester,
Warwick and Huntingdon, go with the king
And take with you free power to ratify,
Augment, or alter, as your wisdoms best

children have lost—or no longer have time to learn—skills that should be a credit to our country. They grow like savages—like soldiers who meditate on nothing but blood—surrounded by swearing and stern looks, ragged clothing and everything unnatural. It's to reverse all this, so we can once again become as we were, that you have all been brought together; therefore I demand to know why gentle peace should not banish these troubles and bless us with her former qualities.

KING HENRY

Duke of Burgundy, if you want peace, the lack of which creates these misfortunes you describe, you must purchase it buy agreeing across-the-board to all our very just demands. You hold the details and particulars of our terms, briefly enumerated, before you in your hands.

BURGUNDY

The king has heard them, but as yet has made no answer.

KING HENRY

Well, the peace you pleaded for so eloquently just now lies in his answer.

KING OF FRANCE

I've only given the articles a cursory glance. If your Grace would kindly appoint some members of your council to sit with me once more and go over them more carefully, I will give my answer and acceptance right away.

KING HENRY

Brother, I shall. Go, uncle Exeter, and brother Clarence, and you, brother Gloucester, Warwick and Huntingdon, go with the king. You have full power to confirm, change, or add to any of my demands in any

Shall see advantageable for our dignity,
Anything in or out of our demands,
And we'll consign thereto.—Will you, fair sister,
Go with the princes or stay here with us?

QUEEN ISABEL
Our gracious brother, I will go with them.
Haply a woman's voice may do some good,
When articles too nicely urged be stood on.

KING HENRY
Yet leave our cousin Katherine here with us.
She is our capital demand, comprised
Within the forerank of our articles.

QUEEN ISABEL
She hath good leave.

Exeunt all except KING HENRY, KATHERINE, *and* ALICE

KING HENRY
Fair Katherine, and most fair,
Will you vouchsafe to teach a soldier terms
Such as will enter at a lady's ear
And plead his love suit to her gentle heart?

KATHERINE
Your Majesty shall mock at me. I cannot speak your England.

KING HENRY
O fair Katherine, if you will love me soundly with your French heart, I will be glad to hear you confess it brokenly with your English tongue. Do you like me, Kate?

KATHERINE
Pardonnez-moi, I cannot tell what is "like me."

KING HENRY
An angel is like you, Kate, and you are like an angel.

KATHERINE
(to ALICE*) Que dit-il? Que je suis semblable à les anges?*

way that you judge advantageous to my rule, and I'll undertake to agree to it. Fair sister, will you go with the princes or stay here with me?

QUEEN ISABEL

Gracious brother, I will go with them. Perhaps a woman's voice may do some good when some small detail proves to be holding things up.

KING HENRY

In that case, leave our cousin Katherine here with us. She is our principal demand—one of the first points of the treaty.

QUEEN ISABEL

She is welcome to stay.

Everyone except KING HENRY, KATHERINE, *and* ALICE *exits.*

KING HENRY

Lovely, most lovely Katherine, will you agree to teach a soldier the words that would recommend his love-suit to a gentle heart like yours?

KATHERINE

Your Majesty shall mock at me. I cannot speak your England.

KING HENRY

Lovely Katherine, if you will love me well with your French heart, I'm happy to hear you confess it in broken English. Do you like me, Kate?

KATHERINE

Pardon me but I do not know what is "like me."

KING HENRY

An angel is like you, Kate, and you are like an angel.

KATHERINE

(*to* ALICE, *in French*) What does he say? That I am like an angel?

ALICE

Oui, vraiment, sauf votre Grâce, ainsi dit-il.

KING HENRY

I said so, dear Katherine; and I must not blush to affirm it.

KATHERINE

Ô bon Dieu! Les langues des hommes sont pleines de tromperies.

KING HENRY

What says she, fair one? That the tongues of men are full of deceits?

ALICE

Oui, dat de tongues of de mans is be full of deceits; dat is de princess.

KING HENRY

The princess is the better Englishwoman.—I' faith, Kate, my wooing is fit for thy understanding. I am glad thou canst speak no better English, for if thou couldst, thou wouldst find me such a plain king that thou wouldst think I had sold my farm to buy my crown. I know no ways to mince it in love, but directly to say, "I love you." Then if you urge me farther than to say, "Do you, in faith?" I wear out my suit. Give me your answer, i' faith, do; and so clap hands and a bargain. How say you, lady?

KATHERINE

Sauf votre honneur, me understand vell.

KING HENRY

Marry, if you would put me to verses or to dance for your sake, Kate, why you undid me. For the one, I have neither words nor measure; and for the other, I have no strength in measure, yet a reasonable measure in strength. If I could win a lady at leapfrog or by vaulting into my saddle with my armor on my back, under the correction of bragging be it spoken, I should quickly leap into a wife. Or if I might buffet for my love or bound my horse for her favors, I could lay on like a butcher and sit like a jackanapes, never off. But,

ALICE

(*in French*) Yes, your Grace, that's what he says.

KING HENRY

I said so, dear Katherine, and I'm not ashamed to repeat it.

KATHERINE

(*in French*) Oh, Lord! The tongues of men are full of deceit.

KING HENRY

(*to* ALICE) What does she say, pretty one? That the tongues of men are full of deceits?

ALICE

Oui, dat de tongues of de mans is be full of deceits: dere's de princess for you.

KING HENRY

How very English of her. Kate, my wooing is fit for your understanding: I amglad your English isn't better. If it were, you would find me such an ordinary king that you would think I'd sold my farm to buy my crown. I don't know any fancy ways of talking about love, only to say right out, "I love you." If you press me any further than with the question, "Do you really?" my love scene is over. So give me your answer, and we'll shake on it. Deal?

KATHERINE

With all due respect, me understand well.

KING HENRY

Really, if you were thinking of having me write poetry or dance for you, Kate, you've defeated me already. I have no gift for the one and no strength for the other, though I have the gift of strength. If I could win a lady by playing leapfrog or vaulting into my saddle with my armor on my back—though you may accuse me of boasting—I could easily get myself a wife. I can fight with my fists and rear my horse up without falling off him, if either of those things could win me love. But, before God, Kate, I cannot look greenly nor gasp out my eloquence, nor I have no cunning in protestation, only downright oaths, which I never use till urged, nor never break for urging. If thou canst love a fellow of this temper, Kate, whose face is not worth sunburning, that never looks in his glass for love of anything he sees there, let thine eye be thy cook. I speak to thee plain soldier. If thou canst love me for this, take me. If not, to say to thee that I shall die is true, but for thy love, by the Lord, no. Yet I love thee too. And while thou liv'st, dear Kate, take a fellow of plain and uncoined constancy, for he perforce must do thee right because he hath not the gift to woo in other places. For these fellows of infinite tongue, that can rhyme themselves into ladies' favors, they do always reason themselves out again. What? A speaker is but a prater, a rhyme is but a ballad, a good leg will fall, a straight back will stoop, a black beard will turn white, a curled pate will grow bald, a fair face will wither, a full eye will wax hollow, but a good heart, Kate, is the sun and the moon, or rather the sun and not the moon, for it shines bright and never changes but keeps his course truly. If thou would have such a one, take me. And take me, take a soldier. Take a soldier, take a king. And what say'st thou then to my love? Speak, my fair, and fairly, I pray thee.

KATHERINE

Is it possible dat I sould love de enemy of France?

KING HENRY

No, it is not possible you should love the enemy of France, Kate. But, in loving me, you should love the friend of France, for I love France so well that I will not part with a village of it. I will have it all mine. And, Kate, when France is mine and I am yours, then yours is France and you are mine.

KATHERINE

I cannot tell wat is dat.

before God, Kate, I cannot turn pale on purpose or gasp out fancy phrases, and I have no gift for clever declarations, only blunt oaths, which I never use till I'm asked and never break no matter who asks me. If you can love a man of this temperament, Kate, whose face a sunburn wouldn't make any worse and who never looks in the mirror to admire himself, let your eye improve me. I speak to you as a plain soldier. If you can love me for this, take me. If not, to tell you I will die is true, but not for love, by God. And yet I do love you. So take for life a fellow of pure and plain faithfulness. He's bound to be true to you as he won't be up to flirting with other women. These chatty fellows who can rhyme their way into a lady's good graces always reason themselves out again. Look, a talker is just a gabber; a poem is just a rhyme. A good leg will shrink, a straight back stoop, a black beard turn white, a curly head grow bald, an attractive face grow wrinkled and a pretty eye hollow. But a good heart, Kate, is the sun and the moon, or, rather, the sun, and not the moon, for it goes on shining brightly forever. If you would have such a man, take me. Take me and get a soldier; take a soldier and get a king. So what do you say to my suit? Speak, my fair one, and speak fairly, I beg you.

KATHERINE

Is it possible dat I sould love de enemy of France?

KING HENRY

No, it is not possible you should love the enemy of France, Kate. But in loving me, you would love the friend of France, for I love France so much that I will not part with a single village of it. I will have it all mine. And, Kate, when France is mine and I am yours, then France is yours and you are mine.

KATHERINE

I don't understand all dat.

KING HENRY

No, Kate? I will tell thee in French, which I am sure will hang upon my tongue like a new-married wife about her husband's neck, hardly to be shook off. Je quand sur le possession de France, et quand vous avez le possession de moi—let me see, what then? Saint Denis be my speed!—donc vôtre est France et vous êtes mienne. It is as easy for me, Kate, to conquer the kingdom as to speak so much more French. I shall never move thee in French, unless it be to laugh at me.

KATHERINE

Sauf votre honneur, le français que vous parlez, il est meilleur que l'anglais lequel je parle.

KING HENRY

No, faith, is 't not, Kate, but thy speaking of my tongue, and I thine, most truly-falsely must needs be granted to be much at one. But, Kate, dost thou understand thus much English? Canst thou love me?

KATHERINE

I cannot tell.

KING HENRY

Can any of your neighbors tell, Kate? I'll ask them. Come, I know thou lovest me; and at night, when you come into your closet, you'll question this gentlewoman about me, and, I know, Kate, you will to her dispraise those parts in me that you love with your heart. But, good Kate, mock me mercifully, the rather, gentle princess, because I love thee cruelly. If ever thou beest mine, Kate, as I have a saving faith within me tells me thou shalt, I get thee with scambling, and thou must therefore needs prove a good soldier-breeder. Shall not thou and I, between Saint Denis and Saint George, compound a boy, half French, half

KING HENRY

No, Kate? I will tell you in French, which I am sure will hang as heavily on my tongue as a newly married wife around her husband's neck, impossible to shake off. (*in stilted French*) I, when, on the possession of France, and when you have the possession of me—(*in English*) let me see, what then? help me, Saint Denis!—(*French again*) then yours is France and you are mine. (*in English*) It would be as easy for me to reconquer the kingdom, Kate, as it would be for me to speak that much French again. I'll never move you in French, except to laugh at me.

KATHERINE

Your French, sir, is better than my English.

KING HENRY

No, really, it's not, Kate. But your speaking my language, and I yours truly-falsely

Sincerely but incorrectly.

comes to pretty much the same thing. Can you understand this much English though, Kate? Could you love me?

KATHERINE

I cannot tell.

KING HENRY

Can any of your neighbors tell, Kate? I'll ask them. Come, I know you love me. And at night, when you go to your bedroom, you'll question this gentlewoman about me and, I know, Kate, you'll criticize those qualities of mine that you secretly love. But mock me gently, dear Kate, because I love you terribly. If I ever win you, Kate, as I have an inkling I will, it won't be without a skirmish—and that suggests you'd make a good mother of soldiers. Shall not you and I together, then, between Saint Denis and Saint George, make a boy, half French, half English, who will go to Con-

English, that shall go to Constantinople and take the Turk by the beard? Shall we not? What say'st thou, my fair flower de luce?

KATHERINE

I do not know dat.

KING HENRY

No, 'tis hereafter to know, but now to promise. Do but now promise, Kate, you will endeavor for your French part of such a boy; and for my English moiety take the word of a king and a bachelor. How answer you, la plus belle *Katherine du monde, mon très cher et divin déesse?*

KATHERINE

Your Majestée ave fausse French enough to deceive de most sage *demoiselle* dat is *en* France.

KING HENRY

Now fie upon my false French. By mine honor, in true English, I love thee, Kate. By which honor I dare not swear thou lovest me, yet my blood begins to flatter me that thou dost, notwithstanding the poor and untempering effect of my visage. Now, beshrew my father's ambition! He was thinking of civil wars when he got me; therefore was I created with a stubborn outside, with an aspect of iron, that when I come to woo ladies, I fright them. But, in faith, Kate, the elder I wax, the better I shall appear. My comfort is that old age, that ill layer-up of beauty, can do no more spoil upon my face. Thou hast me, if thou hast me, at the worst, and thou shalt wear me, if thou wear me, better and better. And therefore tell me, most fair Katherine, will you have me? Put off your maiden blushes, avouch the thoughts of your heart with the looks of an empress, take me by the hand, and say "Harry of England, I am thine," which word thou shalt no sooner bless mine ear withal, but I will tell thee aloud "England is thine, Ireland is thine, France is stantinople and grab the Turk by the beard? Shall we not? What do you say, my fair *fleur-de-lys*?

KATHERINE

I do not know dat.

KING HENRY

No, of course you don't. It lies in the future, along with certainty. Now there can only be the promise. Do promise, Kate, that you'll do your French part to bring forth such a boy; and for my English half, take the word of a king and a bachelor. What's your answer, (*speaking in French*) oh loveliest of Katherines, my most precious and divine goddess?

KATHERINE

Your Majesty has false French enough to deceive de wisest lady in France.

KING HENRY

Damn my false French. I tell you truly, in true English: I love you, Kate. And though I wouldn't dare to swear that you love me, still my blood begins to flatter me that you do, despite the ill effects of my face. Curse my father's ambition! He was thinking of civil wars when he conceived me, and consequently my outward appearance is harsh and steely. I intimidate ladies when I come to woo them. But I promise you, Kate: the older I grow the better I'll look. My comfort is that old age, that poor preserver of beauty, can't make my face any worse than it already is. If you have me, you have me now at my worst; and if you have me, you'll appreciate me better and better. Therefore tell me, fairest Katherine, will you have me? Put aside your maiden blushes and speak your true feelings with the bearing of an empress. Take me by the hand and say, "Harry of England, I am yours." No sooner shall I hear that word than I will tell you straight out, "England is yours, Ireland is yours, France is yours,

thine, and Harry Plantagenet is thine," who, though I speak it before his face, if he be not fellow with the best king, thou shalt find the best king of good fellows. Come, your answer in broken music, for thy voice is music and thy English broken. Therefore, queen of all, Katherine, break thy mind to me in broken English. Wilt thou have me?

KATHERINE
Dat is as it sall please de *roi mon père.*

KING HENRY
Nay, it will please him well, Kate; it shall please him, Kate.

KATHERINE
Den it sall also content me.

KING HENRY
Upon that I kiss your hand, and I call you my queen.

KATHERINE
Laissez, mon seigneur, laissez, laissez! Ma foi, je ne veux point que vous abaissiez votre grandeur en baisant la main d'une—Notre Seigneur!—indigne serviteur. Excusez-moi, je vous supplie, mon très puissant seigneur.

KING HENRY
Then I will kiss your lips, Kate.

KATHERINE
Les dames et demoiselles pour être baisées devant leur noces, il n'est pas la coutume de France.

KING HENRY
Madam my interpreter, what says she?

ALICE
Dat it is not be de fashion pour les ladies of France—I cannot tell wat is *baiser en* Anglish.

KING HENRY
To kiss.

ALICE
Your *Majesté entendre* bettre *que moi.*

and Harry Plantagenet is yours." And, though I say so in his presence, if he's not a friend of the best kings, you'll find him king of the best friends. Come on, tell me in broken music—for your voice is music and your English broken. Come, Katherine Queen of All, reveal your heart to me in broken English. Will you have me?

KATHERINE

Dat is as it shall please de king my father.

KING HENRY

Oh, it will please him, Kate. It will please him very well.

KATHERINE

Den it shall also content me.

KING HENRY

With that I kiss your hand and call you my queen.

KATHERINE

(*in French*) No, sir! Stop, stop! Heavens, I can't allow you to lower yourself by kissing the hand of one of your humble servants. I hope you'll pardon me, mighty king.

KING HENRY

Then I will kiss your lips, Kate.

KATHERINE

(*in French*) It is not the custom for French maidens to kiss before they are married.

KING HENRY

What does she say, madam interpreter?

ALICE

Dat it not be de custom pour les ladies of France—I cannot tell vat is *baiser* en Anglish.

KING HENRY

To kiss.

ALICE

Your Majesty understand bettre den me.

KING HENRY

It is not a fashion for the maids in France to kiss before they are married, would she say?

ALICE

Oui, vraiment.

KING HENRY

O Kate, nice customs curtsy to great kings. Dear Kate, you and I cannot be confined within the weak list of a country's fashion. We are the makers of manners, Kate, and the liberty that follows our places stops the mouth of all find-faults, as I will do yours for upholding the nice fashion of your country in denying me a kiss. Therefore, patiently and yielding. *(kissing her)* You have witchcraft in your lips, Kate. There is more eloquence in a sugar touch of them than in the tongues of the French council, and they should sooner persuade Harry of England than a general petition of monarchs. Here comes your father.

Enter the FRENCH KING, QUEEN ISABEL, BURGUNDY, *and other* LORDS

BURGUNDY

God save your Majesty. My royal cousin, teach you our princess English?

KING HENRY

I would have her learn, my fair cousin, how perfectly I love her, and that is good English.

BURGUNDY

Is she not apt?

KING HENRY

Our tongue is rough, coz, and my condition is not smooth, so that, having neither the voice nor the heart of flattery about me, I cannot so conjure up the spirit of love in her that he will appear in his true likeness.

KING HENRY

It is not the custom for the maids in France to kiss before they are married, is that what she says?

ALICE

Yes, exactly.

KING HENRY

Oh, Kate, prudish customs bow before great kings. You and I cannot be held within the confines of a country's arbitrary customs, dear Kate. You and I, Kate, we are the makers of custom, and the freedom that goes with our position silences all who would criticize, as I will silence you for upholding the prudish custom of your country in refusing me a kiss. Therefore, willingly and yielding. (*kisses her*) You have witchcraft in your lips, Kate. There is more eloquence in a sweet touch of them than in the tongues of the whole French council. They would persuade Harry of England sooner than a whole assembly of monarchs. Here comes your father.

The FRENCH KING *and* QUEEN, BURGUNDY, *and other* LORDS *enter.*

BURGUNDY

God save your Majesty. My royal kinsman, are you teaching our princess English?

KING HENRY

I wanted to teach her how perfectly I love her, kinsman, and that's good English.

BURGUNDY

She picks it up quick, doesn't she?

KING HENRY

Our language is rough, friend, and it's not in my nature to speak smoothly. So, possessing neither a voice nor a heart for flattery, I can't awaken the spirit of love in her so as to make him appear in his true likeness.

BURGUNDY

Pardon the frankness of my mirth if I answer you for that. If you would conjure in her, you must make a circle; if conjure up Love in her in his true likeness, he must appear naked and blind. Can you blame her then, being a maid yet rosed over with the virgin crimson of modesty, if she deny the appearance of a naked blind boy in her naked seeing self? It were, my lord, a hard condition for a maid to consign to.

KING HENRY

Yet they do wink and yield, as love is blind and enforces.

BURGUNDY

They are then excused, my lord, when they see not what they do.

KING HENRY

Then, good my lord, teach your cousin to consent winking.

BURGUNDY

I will wink on her to consent, my lord, if you will teach her to know my meaning, for maids, well summered and warm kept, are like flies at Bartholomew-tide: blind, though they have their eyes; and then they will endure handling, which before would not abide looking on.

KING HENRY

This moral ties me over to time and a hot summer. And so I shall catch the fly, your cousin, in the latter end and she must be blind too.

BURGUNDY

As love is, my lord, before it loves.

KING HENRY

It is so. And you may, some of you, thank love for my blindness, who cannot see many a fair French city for one fair French maid that stands in my way.

FRENCH KING

Yes, my lord, you see them perspectively, the cities turned into a maid, for they are all girdled with maiden walls that war hath never entered.

BURGUNDY

Forgive my boldness if I take you up on your words about making magic. For love to appear in his true likeness, he would have to be as Cupid is: naked and blind. How can you blame her, a tender young maiden still given to virgin blushes, for objecting to having a blind, naked boy appear before her? It's a lot to ask of a maiden.

KING HENRY

But virgins close their eyes and submit all the time, and blind love has his way.

BURGUNDY

They're forgiven, then, if they don't see what they're doing.

KING HENRY

Then teach your cousin to also be willing to close her eyes, my lord.

BURGUNDY

I will signal her with a wink to consent, my lord, if you will teach her what that means. Maidens who are well fed and well taken care of are like August flies, blind though they can see. They'll let you handle them then, though they'd scarcely let you look at them before.

KING HENRY

So you're telling me to give it time and wait for summer. And even then, in order for me to catch the fly your cousin, she must be blind?

BURGUNDY

Like love, my lord, before it learns to love.

KING HENRY

Fair enough. Some of you may, thank love for my blindness. There's many a French town that I can't see because one pretty French maid stands in front of me.

FRENCH KING

Oh yes, my lord, you see them, but you see them metaphorically. The cities appear to you like a maiden because virgin walls, which war has never invaded, surround them.

KING HENRY
Shall Kate be my wife?

FRENCH KING
So please you.

KING HENRY
I am content, so the maiden cities you talk of may wait on her. So the maid that stood in the way for my wish shall show me the way to my will.

FRENCH KING
We have consented to all terms of reason.

KING HENRY
Is 't so, my lords of England?

WESTMORELAND
The king hath granted every article,
His daughter first, and, in sequel, all,
According to their firm proposed natures.

EXETER
Only he hath not yet subscribèd this:
Where your Majesty demands that the king of France, having any occasion to write for matter of grant, shall name your Highness in this form and with this addition, in French: *Notre très cher fils Henri, roi d'Angleterre, héritier de France*; and thus in Latin: *Praeclarissimus filius noster Henricus, rex Angliae, et haeres Franciae.*

FRENCH KING
Nor this I have not, brother, so denied
But your request shall make me let it pass.

KING HENRY
I pray you, then, in love and dear alliance,
Let that one article rank with the rest,
And thereupon give me your daughter.

FRENCH KING
Take her, fair son, and from her blood raise up
Issue to me, that the contending kingdoms
Of France and England, whose very shores look pale
With envy of each other's happiness,

KING HENRY

Shall Kate be my wife?

FRENCH KING

If you wish.

KING HENRY

I am satisfied, as long as the maiden cities you talk of come with her. That way, the maiden that stood between me and them shall be the means of my achieving my desire.

FRENCH KING

We have consented to all reasonable terms.

KING HENRY

Is that true, my lords of England?

WESTMORELAND

The king has agreed to every point: first his daughter, then everything else, as you strictly proposed.

EXETER

Except that he has not yet agreed to address you in this form and with this title—in French, *Notre tres cher fils Henri, Roi d'Angleterre, Heritier de France*; and in Latin, *Praeclarissimus filius noster Henricus, Rex Angliae, et Haeres Franciae.*

"Our thrice-glorious son, Henry, King of England and Heir of France"

FRENCH KING

And even this I'm willing to grant if you request it.

KING HENRY

In that case, I ask that for the sake of friendship and alliance you let that one item stand with the rest, and bestow your daughter on me.

FRENCH KING

Take her, my son, and give me children by her, so that the warring kingdoms of France and England, whose very shores have paled in envy at each other's happiness, may finally end their mutual hostility. May this

May cease their hatred, and this dear conjunction
Plant neighborhood and Christian-like accord
In their sweet bosoms, that never war advance
His bleeding sword 'twixt England and fair France.

LORDS

Amen.

KING HENRY

Now welcome, Kate, and bear me witness all
That here I kiss her as my sovereign queen.

Flourish

QUEEN ISABEL

God, the best maker of all marriages,
Combine your hearts in one, your realms in one.
As man and wife, being two, are one in love,
So be there 'twixt your kingdoms such a spousal
That never may ill office or fell jealousy,
Which troubles oft the bed of blessèd marriage,
Thrust in between the paction of these kingdoms
To make divorce of their incorporate league,
That English may as French, French Englishmen,
Receive each other. God speak this "amen"!

ALL

Amen.

KING HENRY

Prepare we for our marriage; on which day,
My Lord of Burgundy, we'll take your oath,
And all the peers', for surety of our leagues.
Then shall I swear to Kate, and you to me,
And may our oaths well kept and prosp'rous be.

Sennet

Exeunt

precious marriage cause friendship and alliance between them and war never again threaten England or fair France with his bloody sword.

ALL

Amen.

KING HENRY

Now, welcome, Kate.—And let everyone bear witness that here I kiss her as my sovereign queen.

Trumpets sound.

QUEEN ISABEL

May God, who is the best matchmaker, join your hearts and realms in one. As man and wife, though two, are one in love, so let there be between your kingdoms such a marriage that neither wrongdoing nor fierce jealousy, which often trouble the sacred state of marriage, ever sever them. And let Englishmen be French and Frenchmen English. God say, "Amen"!

ALL

Amen!

KING HENRY

Let us prepare for our wedding.—On that day, I'll take your oath of loyalty, my Lord of Burgundy and all my peers, to guarantee my treaty. Then I will swear to Kate and you to me, and may our oaths be faithfully kept and prove fortunate.

Trumpets sound.

They all exit.

EPILOGUE

Enter CHORUS

CHORUS

Thus far with rough and all-unable pen
Our bending author hath pursued the story,
In little room confining mighty men,
Mangling by starts the full course of their glory.
Small time, but in that small most greatly lived
This star of England. Fortune made his sword,
By which the world's best garden be achieved
And of it left his son imperial lord.
Henry the Sixth, in infant bands crowned king
Of France and England, did this king succeed,
Whose state so many had the managing
That they lost France and made his England bleed,
Which oft our stage hath shown. And for their sake,
In your fair minds let this acceptance take.

Exit

EPILOGUE

The CHORUS *enters.*

CHORUS

Thus far has our straining author pursued the story with his crude, inadequate writing, keeping important people penned up in this little room while he mangled history's full glory with his uneven telling. The lifespan of our English hero was brief, but in that brief time he achieved greatness. He had good luck as a warrior, and with it he created the world's greatest garden, France, leaving his son as its imperial ruler. Henry the Sixth, crowned king of France and England while still in his infancy, succeeded him. But so many people had a hand in managing the child's kingdom that France was lost and civil war came to England—a story we've acted out many times on this stage. With those plays in mind, we hope you'll receive this one kindly.

The CHORUS *exits.*

SPARKNOTES™ LITERATURE GUIDES

1984
The Adventures of Huckleberry Finn
The Adventures of Tom Sawyer
The Aeneid
All Quiet on the Western Front
And Then There Were None
Angela's Ashes
Animal Farm
Anna Karenina
Anne of Green Gables
Anthem
Antony and Cleopatra
Aristotle's Ethics
As I Lay Dying
As You Like It
Atlas Shrugged
The Autobiography of Malcolm X
The Awakening
The Bean Trees
The Bell Jar
Beloved
Beowulf
Billy Budd
Black Boy
Bless Me, Ultima
The Bluest Eye
Brave New World
The Brothers Karamazov
The Call of the Wild
Candide
The Canterbury Tales
Catch-22
The Catcher in the Rye
The Chocolate War
The Chosen
Cold Mountain
Cold Sassy Tree
The Color Purple
The Count of Monte Cristo
Crime and Punishment
The Crucible
Cry, the Beloved Country
Cyrano de Bergerac
David Copperfield
Death of a Salesman
The Death of Socrates
The Diary of a Young Girl
A Doll's House
Don Quixote
Dr. Faustus
Dr. Jekyll and Mr. Hyde
Dracula
Dune
Edith Hamilton's Mythology
Emma
Ethan Frome
Fahrenheit 451
Fallen Angels
A Farewell to Arms
Farewell to Manzanar
Flowers for Algernon
For Whom the Bell Tolls
The Fountainhead
Frankenstein
The Giver
The Glass Menagerie
Gone With the Wind
The Good Earth
The Grapes of Wrath
Great Expectations
The Great Gatsby
Greek Classics
Grendel
Gulliver's Travels
Hamlet
The Handmaid's Tale
Hard Times
Harry Potter and the Sorcerer's Stone
Heart of Darkness
Henry IV, Part I
Henry V
Hiroshima
The Hobbit
The House of Seven Gables
I Know Why the Caged Bird Sings
The Iliad
Inferno
Inherit the Wind
Invisible Man
Jane Eyre
Johnny Tremain
The Joy Luck Club
Julius Caesar
The Jungle
The Killer Angels
King Lear
The Last of the Mohicans
Les Miserables
A Lesson Before Dying
The Little Prince
Little Women
Lord of the Flies
The Lord of the Rings
Macbeth
Madame Bovary
A Man for All Seasons
The Mayor of Casterbridge
The Merchant of Venice
A Midsummer Night's Dream
Moby Dick
Much Ado About Nothing
My Antonia
Narrative of the Life of Frederick Douglass
Native Son
The New Testament
Night
Notes from Underground
The Odyssey
The Oedipus Plays
Of Mice and Men
The Old Man and the Sea
The Old Testament
Oliver Twist
The Once and Future King
One Day in the Life of Ivan Denisovich
One Flew Over the Cuckoo's Nest
One Hundred Years of Solitude
Othello
Our Town
The Outsiders
Paradise Lost
A Passage to India
The Pearl
The Picture of Dorian Gray
Poe's Short Stories
A Portrait of the Artist as a Young Man
Pride and Prejudice
The Prince
A Raisin in the Sun
The Red Badge of Courage
The Republic
Richard III
Robinson Crusoe
Romeo and Juliet
The Scarlet Letter
A Separate Peace
Silas Marner
Sir Gawain and the Green Knight
Slaughterhouse-Five
Snow Falling on Cedars
Song of Solomon
The Sound and the Fury
Steppenwolf
The Stranger
Streetcar Named Desire
The Sun Also Rises
A Tale of Two Cities
The Taming of the Shrew
The Tempest
Tess of the d'Ubervilles
The Things They Carried
Their Eyes Were Watching God
Things Fall Apart
To Kill a Mockingbird
To the Lighthouse
Treasure Island
Twelfth Night
Ulysses
Uncle Tom's Cabin
Walden
War and Peace
Wuthering Heights
A Yellow Raft in Blue Water